NTC SKILL BUILDERS

W9-BHJ-127

WHAT YOU NEED TO KNOW ABOUT

DEVELOPING YOUR TEST-TAKING SKILLS: STANDARD ENGLISH

Robert S. Boone

Printed on recyclable paper

 VGM Career Horizons
a division of *NTC Publishing Group*
Lincolnwood, Illinois USA

Published by VGM Career Horizons, a division of NTC Publishing Group.
© 1996 by NTC Publishing Group, 4255 West Touhy Avenue,
Lincolnwood (Chicago), Illinois 60646-1975 U.S.A.
Manufactured in the United States of America.
Library of Congress Card Catalog Number 95-61815

5 6 7 8 9 VP 0 9 8 7 6 5 4 3 2 1

Contents

Standard English

Vocabulary

Grammar and Usage

Vocabulary

INTRODUCTION

Of the many standardized tests you will take before entering college, vocabulary tests will predominate. Some college entrance examinations and state standardized tests measure vocabulary knowledge, and colleges often use vocabulary test results to help determine a student's placement level for English. This unit will prepare you for typical vocabulary tests.

Beyond excelling on vocabulary tests, however, there are other benefits to expanding and strengthening your knowledge of words. Obviously, knowledge of vocabulary will be helpful in taking *any* standardized test because all such tests involve language. In particular, the SAT II (achievement tests) assumes that you have a rich vocabulary, and, although the ACT does not have a specific vocabulary component, the ACT readings themselves include many challenging words. Further, think of your vocabulary as a reflection of what you have learned. To acquire new words is to understand more of your world and to allow more sophisticated, subtle expression of feelings. Clearly, the concepts you learn here for enriching your vocabulary do not have application limited to achievement test preparation. Making a commitment to helping your vocabulary grow is worth doing. You will benefit from your efforts not only in school but throughout your life.

This unit includes twelve Vocabulary Builder Lessons presented in a format designed to equip you to *use* the words you learn. Following these lessons are seven Practice Tests including vocabulary from the twelve lessons. The chapter concludes with seven comprehensive Vocabulary Lists—words that appear most frequently on standardized vocabulary tests.

VOCABULARY BUILDER LESSONS

Here are the sixty words you will be studying in the Vocabulary Builder Lessons.

adroit	despot	peccadillo
ameliorate	dilettante	pedant
amorphous	dominion	perfunctory
ascetic	empirical	periphery
banal	emulate	philanthropist
benumb	enigma	pragmatic
blasé	ephemeral	rationalize
blasphemy	esoteric	sagacity
broach	fallacious	sardonic
cajole	foment	sedition
candor	fortuitous	sinuous
castigate	iconoclast	specious
charlatan	impious	stolid
chauvinism	latent	supercilious
chicanery	malign	sycophant
circumspect	mendacity	synthesize
conjure	misanthrope	truculent
covert	mollify	upbraid
credulous	mundane	verbosity
culpable	oracle	voracious

In each of the Vocabulary Builder Lessons, you will be given a list of five words. Begin by studying each word individually. First, use "Look it over" to observe the word used in different ways and, sometimes, in different forms. Next, in "Write your definition," write down what you think the word means. Then check your definition in a dictionary. Finally, "Apply it" by writing a paragraph or a short essay.

Vocabulary Builder Lesson 1

candor
despot
emulate
ephemeral
esoteric

candor

Look it over.

I thought she would speak with *candor*, but the politician gave evasive answers to the reporter's questions.

Mr. Kim's *candor* at the meeting last night moved the school board to accept his proposal.

I wish she wouldn't always speak with such embarrassing *candor*.

Write your definition. Then check it in the dictionary.

Apply it.

When your best friend asks your opinion of his or her hairstyle, should you respond with *candor*? Why or why not?

Children speak with *candor* that is sometimes refreshing and sometimes amusing. Describe a situation in which your *candor* as a child was humorous, embarrassing, or otherwise memorable.

despot

Look it over.

Demanding and strict, Mr. Velasquez is a *despot* in the classroom.

After reading horrifying accounts of his calculated cruelty, I'm convinced that Hitler was the most infamous *despot* of all.

On the basketball court, Coach Pareli is a *despot* known for his intimidating tirades against the referees and his own players.

Write your definition. Then check it in the dictionary.

Apply it.

Do you think that a *despot* makes an effective leader? Is such a style of leadership ever appropriate? Explain your answers.

What professions or roles encourage people to act like *despots*?

emulate

Look it over.

Young people like to *emulate* Michael Jordan and other popular athletes.

We all need role models to *emulate*.

We are flattered if people *emulate* us.

Write your definition. Then check it in the dictionary.

Apply it.

Whom did you *emulate* as a child? Why?

Do you *emulate* the appearance or behaviors of your peers? Which styles of dress or patterns of behavior do you find yourself adopting? Explain your answer.

ephemeral

Look it over.

The brilliant colors and ear-splitting sounds of the fireworks display were *ephemeral*, but the smoke hung in the air long afterward.

He thought their love would last a lifetime, but it was only *ephemeral*.

He hoped the throbbing pain of the headache would be *ephemeral*.

Write your definition. Then check it in the dictionary.

Apply it.

Which *ephemeral* displays of nature do you find most beau-
tiful? Write vivid descriptions of two of your favorites.

Which *ephemeral* qualities of childhood will you miss most
as an adult? Explain your answer.

esoteric

Look it over.

Juan was mystified by the *esoteric* theorems the mathema-
ticians were discussing excitedly.

Choon spends her time studying *esoteric* subjects such as
Zoroastrianism.

The librarian advised me that my research topic was
esoteric and suggested that I choose a topic with broad
appeal instead.

Write your definition. Then check it in the dictionary.

Apply it.

What once seemed *esoteric* to you that now seems quite
ordinary?

Would you consider rap to be an *esoteric* style of music?
Explain your answer.

Vocabulary Builder Lesson 2

enigma
mollify
pedant
pragmatic
specious

enigma

Look it over.

Jerry is a real *enigma*; we can never guess what he is
thinking.

I expected the problem to be an *enigma,* but we solved it
right away.

The *enigmatic* expression on Ms. James's face made it
difficult to guess her reaction to our proposal.

Write your definition. Then check it in the dictionary.

Apply it.

For some students, a theorem in geometry is baffling. Other
students might comprehend it easily, but they flounder in
applying rules of grammar. Discuss an *enigma* you encountered recently in your schoolwork.

Describe someone you know who is *enigmatic*.

mollify

Look it over.

We tried to *mollify* the hysterical girl.

The manager doubted her ability to *mollify* the furious
customer.

The young mother tried to *mollify* her disappointed toddler.

Write your definition. Then check it in the dictionary.

Apply it.

How did people *mollify* you when you cried as a child?

Suppose, as director of your school play, you had to *mollify* students who tried out but didn't get parts. What would you say to those students? Write your answer.

pedant

Look it over.

Jamie and Ricardo are such *pedants* that they try to turn every conversation into a trivia quiz.

I thought she was just a *pedant,* but she's got good ideas, too.

The *pedantic* professor droned on and on about all the awards he had won in graduate school.

Write your definition. Then check it in the dictionary.

Apply it.

In a television sitcom, how might a teenage *pedant* be portrayed? Describe his or her style of clothing, speech, and the reactions of peers to him or her.

Does a *pedant* make an inspiring or effective teacher? Explain your answer.

pragmatic

Look it over.

He did well in school, but it was at work that he learned to be *pragmatic.*

She had a very *pragmatic,* matter-of-fact approach to problem solving.

The idealistic teen had no interest in anything *pragmatic.*

Write your definition. Then check it in the dictionary.

Apply it.

How can an impulsive person learn to be more *pragmatic*? Describe the most *pragmatic* person you know.

specious

Look it over.

> He thinks it's a legitimate argument, but I consider it *specious*.
>
> It's *specious* to say that you can lose weight on a diet of pizza and chocolate.
>
> Her *specious* argument was believable enough to convince everyone of her innocence.

Write your definition. Then check it in the dictionary.

Apply it.

> What's the most *specious* argument you have ever heard?
>
> How can consumers be taught to see through *specious* product claims?

Vocabulary Builder Lesson 3

blasé
castigate
chicanery
stolid
sycophant

blasé

Look it over.

I thought he would cheer and shout, but instead he acted *blasé* during the whole game.

Mr. Jones finds that enthusiastic teenagers make better babysitters than do *blasé* adults.

As a child she loved to lick the cake frosting from the mixer beaters, but as a *blasé* teenager, she considers it immature to do so.

Write your definition. Then check it in the dictionary.

Apply it.

How would you persuade a *blasé* teenager to dine at your fast-food restaurant? Describe the menu, the decor, and the music in your unique establishment.

Are you *blasé* about celebrating your birthday? What type of celebration do you most enjoy? Why?

castigate

Look it over.

The teacher *castigated* the boy for cheating on the test.

The board members *castigated* the contractor for completing the construction two months late and over budget.

Joel always *castigates* others instead of taking the blame himself.

Write your definition. Then check it in the dictionary.

Apply it.

Should a parent *castigate* a child for a poor report card? Under what circumstances, if any, would it be appropriate to do so? Write your answer.

For what behaviors do you *castigate* yourself?

chicanery

Look it over.

The boss was guilty of *chicanery* when he lied to his workers.

Tell me directly instead of practicing *chicanery* behind my back.

The manufacturer's guarantee of whiter teeth in minutes was only *chicanery*.

Write your definition. Then check it in the dictionary.

Apply it.

As a child, what kind of *chicanery* did you practice to avoid doing chores?

What well-known cartoon characters practice *chicanery?* Describe some typical examples of your favorite characters' actions.

stolid

Look it over.

He was so *stolid* he did not even cry when his cat died.

The military teaches recruits to be *stolid*.

The children pleaded for more dessert but could not persuade their *stolid* parents.

Write your definition. Then check it in the dictionary.

Apply it.

Recall the last time you read a sad book or watched a tearjerker movie or television program. Were you *stolid* throughout? Briefly describe the sad circumstances and your reaction to them.

For what kinds of jobs are *stolid* people best suited? Explain your answer.

sycophant

Look it over.

The king needed *sycophants* to tell him what he wanted to hear.

Challenge her snide criticisms and don't be such a *sycophant!*

Just because I agree with her all the time doesn't mean that I am a *sycophant.*

Write your definition. Then check it in the dictionary.

Apply it.

Describe a time that you felt like a *sycophant.* Discuss the circumstances and how you felt about them.

Describe someone you know who seems to need to be surrounded by *sycophants.* Why do you think this is so?

Vocabulary Builder Lesson 4

ascetic
conjure
malign
perfunctory
sardonic

ascetic

Look it over.

Ascetics don't indulge themselves.
If he's not an *ascetic,* why has he given up all earthly pleasures?
The *ascetic* and the pleasure seeker have little in common.

Write your definition. Then check it in the dictionary.

Apply it.

Could lifestyles in our society be described as *ascetic*? Explain your answer.
Is life simpler for someone who is an *ascetic*? Why or why not?

conjure

Look it over.

In stunned amazement, we watched the magician *conjure* up a ham sandwich.
Before I stand in front of the class to give an oral presentation, I *conjure* up images of classmates eagerly applauding my speech.
Before writing poetry, Suraji tries to *conjure* up powerful images of nature.

Write your definition. Then check it in the dictionary.

Apply it.

What emotions does the smell of freshly baked chocolate chip cookies *conjure* up in you? Describe the scene and how it makes you feel.

What mental pictures of first grade can you *conjure* up? Write a description, including details about the playground, the classroom, your teacher, and your classmates.

malign

Look it over.

I thought you were going to *malign* my homemade muffins, but instead you complimented me on my baking.

If you *malign* people, you will have few friends.

Throughout the campaign, he claimed that he did not intend to *malign* the mayor's character.

Write your definition. Then check it in the dictionary.

Apply it.

Consider the following statement: To *malign* someone is to offer constructive criticism of him or her. Do you agree with this statement? Why or why not?

Is it possible to *malign* someone in a good-natured way? Explain your answer.

perfunctory

Look it over.

The audience was disappointed by the dance company's *perfunctory* performance.

We want a sincere and inspired effort, not a *perfunctory* attempt.

If you want to be pleased with your woodworking project, don't assemble the pieces in a *perfunctory* manner.

Write your definition. Then check it in the dictionary.

Apply it.

How do you respond when a brother, a sister, or a friend handles something that is precious to you in a *perfunctory* manner?

In what professions would it be dangerous to carry out responsibilities in a *perfunctory* manner? Who could be endangered, and how?

sardonic

Look it over.

His *sardonic* expression conveyed his lack of faith in me.

Their *sardonic* comments made me wish I hadn't performed in the talent show.

She could handle constructive criticism, but *sardonic* insults made her cringe.

Write your definition. Then check it in the dictionary.

Apply it.

How do you feel when you make *sardonic* remarks? When someone makes them about you?

Who are some *sardonic* people you have encountered in books or in movies? Describe their appearance, their attitudes, and the reactions of others toward them.

Vocabulary Builder Lesson 5

blasphemy
charlatan
culpable
rationalize
truculent

blasphemy

Look it over.

Many thought his critical comments of the church were
blasphemy.

It's *blasphemy* to belittle the sport of bowling when my dad
is within earshot.

The senior employees regarded the proposed changes to the
company bylaws as *blasphemy.*

Write your definition. Then check it in the dictionary.

Apply it.

Relate an example of *blasphemy* you have learned about in
history class.

How might a vandal be guilty of *blasphemy*? Explain your
answer.

charlatan

Look it over.

I thought he was genuine, but he's only a *charlatan.*

In one well-known musical, a *charlatan* claiming to be a
music professor sells band instruments to the towns-
people.

The *charlatan* duped the elderly woman, disappearing with
all her savings.

Write your definition. Then check it in the dictionary.

Apply it.

Describe a *charlatan* you have encountered.
Who are some well-known *charlatans* in history? How did they draw the public into their schemes?

culpable

Look it over.

The jury must decide whether she is *culpable* of committing that horrible crime.
The students who did not turn in the cheater were as *culpable* as he was.
The *culpable* students eventually confessed their involvement in the vandalism.

Write your definition. Then check it in the dictionary.

Apply it.

How can we be legally innocent but morally *culpable*?
To what extent are parents *culpable* for their children's crimes?

rationalize

Look it over.

Leon tried to *rationalize* his failing grade by describing it as a growing experience.
Don't *rationalize* your failure to participate by claiming to suffer from headaches.
Roberto's behavior at the party was so inconsiderate that even he couldn't *rationalize* his actions.

Write your definition. Then check it in the dictionary.

Apply it.

Suppose you are a newly elected politician who must *rationalize* your stand against building a larger football stadium. Write a press release on this topic.

How might an undeserving child *rationalize* a request for a
   raise in allowance? Write a brief response.

truculent

Look it over.

Only the most *truculent* warriors were chosen to serve in
   the dictator's army.
The *truculent* prizefighter punched viciously at his opponent.
Maybe a peaceful week on the islands will make Bruno less
   truculent.

Write your definition. Then check it in the dictionary.

Apply it.

Which sports encourage *truculent* participants?
Does violence in movies and on television promote *truculent*
   behavior in our society? Explain your answer.

Vocabulary Builder Lesson 6

credulous
foment
misanthrope
verbosity
voracious

credulous

Look it over.

You're so *credulous* you would believe anything that phony says.

Embarrassed by her *credulous* nature, Juanita chose not to discuss the loss of her savings.

He has the reputation of being *credulous,* but in reality he is a skeptic.

Write your definition. Then check it in the dictionary.

Apply it.

Describe a *credulous* cartoon or sitcom character.

Would banking or law enforcement be good professions for *credulous* people? Why or why not?

foment

Look it over.

Did this mutiny happen spontaneously, or was it *fomented*?

The agitator *fomented* a riot of the prisoners.

The soldier began spreading rumors, seeking to *foment* an uprising within the king's armies.

Write your definition. Then check it in the dictionary.

Apply it.

Do union leaders sometimes *foment* labor strikes? Explain your answer.

Describe conditions in which you would allow yourself to be roused to action by a *fomenter*. How could the needs of the public be served by a *fomenter*?

misanthrope

Look it over.

The *misanthrope* rudely slammed the door on the volunteers who were collecting money for charity.

Despite the cruise director's repeated invitations to join in the group activities, the *misanthrope* remained in his stateroom.

The *misanthrope* sought a career in which he could avoid contact with people.

Write your definition. Then check it in the dictionary.

Apply it.

Describe a *misanthrope* you have encountered in literature. What experiences could turn someone into a *misanthrope*?

verbosity

Look it over.

His *verbosity* made it impossible to address all the items on the committee's agenda.

Neal will never be accused of *verbosity,* because he rarely contributes to a conversation.

The pastor's *verbose* sermons on Sunday mornings seemed endless to the children, who sat fidgeting in the church pews.

Write your definition. Then check it in the dictionary.

Apply it.

How does an audience typically react to a speaker's *verbosity*? What sort of body language might the audience exhibit?

Describe a *verbose* person you know.

●
voracious

Look it over.

> Carmen has a *voracious* appetite for science fiction novels, reading all that she can find.
>
> As a child he displayed a *voracious* interest in baseball cards, filling shoebox after shoebox with his growing collection.
>
> His *voracious* hunger for pizza was apparent as he began eating a fifth slice.

Write your definition. Then check it in the dictionary.

Apply it.

> Describe a *voracious* interest or appetite of yours.
>
> What *voracious* appetites or interests do you see displayed by adults in our society? Explain your answer.

Vocabulary Builder Lesson 7

cajole
iconoclast
mendacity
supercilious
synthesize

cajole

Look it over.

We tried to *cajole* Dad into giving us the car for the weekend.

Murali's teacher cannot be *cajoled* into postponing tests.

If you make a demand, he'll refuse, but you might try to *cajole* him.

Write your definition. Then check it in the dictionary.

Apply it.

How would you go about trying to *cajole* a parent to extend your Friday night curfew?

Describe someone you know who is easy to *cajole*.

iconoclast

Look it over.

As a youth in college he was an *iconoclast,* often questioning his family's lifestyle and values.

Ivan's *iconoclastic* thinking led me to reexamine my position on the issue.

Always an *iconoclast,* Susan writes letters to the editor criticizing the actions of the school board.

Write your definition. Then check it in the dictionary.

Apply it.

Discuss an *iconoclast* who has shaped history.

Do you regard yourself as an *iconoclastic* thinker? Why or why not?

mendacity

Look it over.

I thought she always told the truth, but apparently she is capable of *mendacity*.

Jim looked so earnest and convincing that his friends could never tell whether he was guilty of *mendacity*.

Pinocchio's *mendacity* caused his nose to grow longer.

Write your definition. Then check it in the dictionary.

Apply it.

Are there situations in which *mendacity* is excusable? Explain your answer.

Do you think *mendacity* in our society is on the rise? Give examples to support your answer.

supercilious

Look it over.

The *supercilious* attitude of the elegantly dressed salesperson suited the expensive boutique in which she worked.

The *supercilious* art critic sneered at the amateur artists' entries in the show.

I felt intimidated by the *supercilious* patrons and the haughty waiters who seemed amused by my discomfort.

Write your definition. Then check it in the dictionary.

Apply it.

Do *supercilious* people get more attention or faster service in stores and restaurants? Why or why not?

Describe a character from movies or literature who is *supercilious*. How do other characters react to him or her?

synthesize

Look it over.

After you collect the ingredients, *synthesize* them to create a
delicious casserole.

A gifted writer, she can *synthesize* innocence, deceit, and
cunning to create unforgettable stories.

He was a skilled reporter who could *synthesize* facts from a
number of sources.

Write your definition. Then check it in the dictionary.

Apply it.

What ingredients would you *synthesize* to create the topping
for your favorite pizza?

Do chemistry sets and jigsaw puzzles require you to *synthesize*? Explain your answer.

Vocabulary Builder Lesson 8

banal
chauvinism
fallacious
peccadillo
upbraid

banal

Look it over.

Irina complained that the movie she rented from the video store had a *banal* plot, completely lacking in originality.

Bored by the *banal* verses she'd read on the birthday cards sold at the store, Mariko decided to create her own card.

Mr. Patel encouraged his students to avoid using *banal* adjectives in their writing and to turn to a thesaurus for alternatives.

Write your definition. Then check it in the dictionary.

Apply it.

Write a brief description of a friend, using *banal* adjectives to describe his or her clothing, personality, and facial features. Then rewrite the description, substituting fresher, more colorful language.

Contrast something you consider to be *banal* with something else that you view as fresh and original. Explain why you chose those particular examples.

chauvinism

Look it over.

His *chauvinism* blinded him to the weaknesses of his teammates.

Her *chauvinistic* attitude about her college sorority prevented her from recognizing the value of other campus social groups.

In many professions, male *chauvinism* continues to block the hiring and promoting of capable, qualified women.

Write your definition. Then check it in the dictionary.

Apply it.

How is *chauvinism* like prejudice? Explain your answer. Do you think *chauvinism* exists in your school? In what ways?

fallacious

Look it over.

I thought the argument was valid, but my attorney advised me that it was *fallacious.*

After completing the logic course, Maria made very few *fallacious* assertions.

Manufacturers can be held liable for making *fallacious* claims about the performance of a product.

Write your definition. Then check it in the dictionary.

Apply it.

Describe a time when you were deceived by a *fallacious* claim. What was your response?

Should the government protect consumers from *fallacious* claims by manufacturers, or should the buyer take responsibility for products he or she purchases?

peccadillo

Look it over.

He was outraged that a mere *peccadillo* brought him a prison sentence.

Ramon viewed his own tardiness as a *peccadillo,* but his teacher saw this behavior as proof that he is inconsiderate and irresponsible.

Jaywalking is regarded by most citizens as a *peccadillo.*

Write your definition. Then check it in the dictionary.

Apply it.

Would you regard cheating in school as a *peccadillo* or a serious offense? Justify your answer.

What determines whether an act is judged as a *peccadillo*?

upbraid

Look it over.

Instead of *upbraiding* her players for missing scoring opportunities, Coach Alvarez emphasized the positive aspects of the team's performance.

Rocky *upbraided* himself for forgetting the dental appointment.

In the story, the stern governess *upbraided* the children for their mischief and pranks.

Write your definition. Then check it in the dictionary.

Apply it.

Is it good coaching strategy to *upbraid* players for mistakes made in a game? Why or why not?

Does *upbraiding* a child for poor schoolwork help him or her improve academically? Explain your answer.

Vocabulary Builder Lesson 9

ameliorate
dilettante
latent
mundane
sedition

ameliorate

Look it over.

Despite his offer of ice cream and candy, José could not *ameliorate* his young sister's disappointment.

By scrubbing, polishing, painting, and waxing, we did our best to *ameliorate* the damage caused by years of neglect.

The administration uses staggered lunch hours to *ameliorate* the long lines and crowded tables in the school cafeteria.

Write your definition. Then check it in the dictionary.

Apply it.

Describe an action students in your school could take to *ameliorate* an ongoing problem.

Do you think that eating a low-fat diet and exercising regularly can *ameliorate* general health? Why or why not?

dilettante

Look it over.

When it comes to art collecting, Kendra used to be a *dilettante*, but now she has grown serious about the activity.

I thought that Sean was an expert in this field, but he is only a *dilettante*.

A *dilettante* would not be able to solve this complex problem.

Write your definition. Then check it in the dictionary.

Apply it.

In what areas might you be considered a *dilettante*?

Discuss a character from literature or television who is a *dilettante* detective. How is he or she portrayed—capable or fumbling?

●
latent

Look it over.

Who could have guessed that such a soft-spoken man would possess *latent* musical talent?

Education should help students' *latent* strengths emerge.

Some professionals are better than others at spotting *latent* talents in children.

Write your definition. Then check it in the dictionary.

Apply it.

Choose a favorite poem or song lyrics and discuss their *latent* meaning.

How can teachers draw out a student's *latent* abilities?

●
mundane

Look it over.

He wanted to experience an exciting adventure, not take a *mundane* tour.

What some people find thrilling others consider *mundane*.

After I broke my arm, I found even *mundane* household chores were difficult to perform.

Write your definition. Then check it in the dictionary.

Apply it.

What task or activity that fascinated you as a child do you now regard as *mundane?*

Which tasks seem *mundane* when done alone, but entertaining when done with a friend?

sedition

Look it over.

During the 1960s, many considered student anti-war protests to be *seditious*.

In the former Soviet Union, many anti-Communist writers were convicted and imprisoned for *sedition*.

Our history teacher jokingly accused us of *sedition* when we complained about the surprise quiz.

Write your definition. Then check it in the dictionary.

Apply it.

In the business world, should union organizing be regarded as *sedition*? Explain your answer.

Do you consider *sedition* a serious offense? Why or why not?

Vocabulary Builder Lesson 10

benumb
dominion
empirical
impious
oracle

benumb

Look it over.

Instead of being stimulated by the book, Gabriel was *benumbed.*
Maria was *benumbed* after working in the hot sun all day.
Five straight hours of standardized tests had *benumbed* the students.

Write your definition. Then check it in the dictionary.

Apply it.

What experiences *benumb* you?
When is it convenient to become *benumbed*?

dominion

Look it over.

As the dictator grew more feeble, his *dominion* lessened.
Historians still marvel at the extent of Alexander the Great's *dominion*.
Street gangs refer to their *dominion* as "turf."

Write your definition. Then check it in the dictionary.

Apply it.

In what areas of their lives do most teenagers have little *dominion*?
Write a fantasy in which you reign as king or queen. Describe your *dominion*.

empirical

Look it over.

> A scientist must rely on *empirical* knowledge rather than intuition.
>
> Natasha checked the dashboard gauges but could find no *empirical* evidence that something was wrong.
>
> He made decisions according to his instincts, paying little attention to *empirical* knowledge.

Write your definition. Then check it in the dictionary.

Apply it.

> Do you rely more on *empirical* knowledge or intuition when making a decision? Why?
>
> Is the result of research always *empirical* knowledge?

impious

Look it over.

> Harlan's *impious* nature made him an unlikely choice for altar boy.
>
> Mom and Dad say they are unhappy with my *impious* attitude toward my grandfather.
>
> The students discussed the meaning of the *impious* lyrics on the rock group's latest recording.

Write your definition. Then check it in the dictionary.

Apply it.

> What kinds of events can suddenly change an *impious* person's way of thinking?
>
> Is the commercialization of religious holidays such as Christmas and Easter *impious*?

●

oracle

Look it over.

> In the myth, the king visited an *oracle* to learn the intentions of the gods.
>
> Like an *oracle*, Antonio could always predict the winner of big football games.
>
> Tiffany's reputation as a Wall Street *oracle* led many people to take her investment advice.

Write your definition. Then check it in the dictionary.

Apply it.

> In what areas are you considered an *oracle*?
>
> Describe how you might use your gifts as an *oracle* to improve society.

Vocabulary Builder Lesson 11

broach
circumspect
fortuitous
periphery
sagacity

broach

Look it over.

Sarah was too embarrassed to *broach* such a personal subject.

When you *broached* the idea of job sharing, I was quite surprised.

The talk show host *broached* the delicate subject, then called for a commercial break.

Write your definition. Then check it in the dictionary.

Apply it.

How do various television talk show hosts differ in the styles they use to *broach* serious subjects?

As a dedicated and capable employee, how would you go about *broaching* the subject of a request for a raise in salary?

circumspect

Look it over.

Jamo was impulsive, while his brother was more *circumspect*.

Several bad experiences taught Meechi to be *circumspect*.

Sometimes you must act quickly because there is no time to be *circumspect*.

Write your definition. Then check it in the dictionary.

Apply it.

In what areas do you wish you were more *circumspect*? Why?

How might you teach a child to be *circumspect* with regard to strangers?

fortuitous

Look it over.

It was *fortuitous* that Joni stepped off of the elevator just before the power failed.

How *fortuitous* that the lottery ticket you found is a winning ticket!

It would be *fortuitous* if you found you were seated next to a friend on the airplane.

Write your definition. Then check it in the dictionary.

Apply it.

Describe a *fortuitous* event in your life.

Do you believe that events in life can be *fortuitous*, or is everything that happens predestined to occur?

periphery

Look it over.

You guard the courtyard while I check out the *periphery* of the hotel.

Some children like to skate in the center of the ice rink, while others race around the *periphery*.

The rectangular *periphery* of the swimming pool was patterned in colorful ceramic tile.

Write your definition. Then check it in the dictionary.

Apply it.

Are your opinions typical of your age group, or do you stand on the *periphery*?

Describe your design for the *periphery* of a city park with a fountain in the center.

●

sagacity

Look it over.

The general used *sagacity* and cunning in devising brilliant
military strategies.
A *sagacious* businessman, he made profitable investments.
She plans each move on the chess board with *sagacity*.

Write your definition. Then check it in the dictionary.

Apply it.

For which professions is *sagacity* an essential quality?
Does *sagacity* develop with maturity and experience?
Explain your answer.

Vocabulary Builder Lesson 12

adroit
amorphous
covert
philanthropist
sinuous

adroit

Look it over.

The *adroit* movements of the magician's hands fascinated us.
Moving quickly through the crowd, the celebrity *adroitly*
    maneuvered her way to a waiting limousine.
Marisa's fingers raced *adroitly* across the computer keyboard.

Write your definition. Then check it in the dictionary.

Apply it.

What professions require people to be *adroit*?
Picture yourself as a gymnast competing in the Olympics.
    Describe your *adroit* performance on the parallel bars.

amorphous

Look it over.

She claimed to see a horse and a dog as she studied the sky,
    but he saw only *amorphous* clouds.
No longer shaped like stars, the cookies had melted into an
    amorphous mass in the overheated oven.
The newspaper editor turned his *amorphous* ramblings into
    a concise account of the accident.

Write your definition. Then check it in the dictionary.

Apply it.

You are to design a sculpture for a modern art display. De-
    scribe your *amorphous* creation and the materials from
    which it is made.

Are your thoughts sometimes *amorphous,* or are they always clear and distinct?

covert

Look it over.

The CIA carries out *covert* investigations.
He wanted to be an undercover detective so he could participate in *covert* operations.
The police uncovered the *covert* gambling establishment.

Write your definition. Then check it in the dictionary.

Apply it.

Briefly describe a book or movie concerned with a *covert* organization.
Why are some people fascinated by *covert* operations?

philanthropist

Look it over.

The *philanthropist* donated millions of dollars to worthy causes.
Rockefeller and Carnegie were well-known American *philanthropists.*
The new theater group was looking to a *philanthropist* for help with funding.

Write your definition. Then check it in the dictionary.

Apply it.

How is your life affected by *philanthropists*?
As a *philanthropist,* which worthy causes would you choose to support?

●

sinuous

Look it over.

> The icy weather made the twisting, *sinuous* road especially dangerous.
>
> The *sinuous* threads of gold and silver were interwoven in a delicate chain.
>
> The artist added light, *sinuous* lines to contrast with her bold, straight strokes.

Write your definition. Then check it in the dictionary.

Apply it.

> Describe a *sinuous* path or road you have traveled.
>
> Mysteries often have *sinuous* plots to keep the reader guessing. Describe the sinuous plot of a book you have read.

VOCABULARY PRACTICE TESTS

Test makers measure your understanding of vocabulary terms in a variety of ways. On the pages that follow you will find examples of seven different vocabulary tests. These tests include the words you studied previously in the twelve Vocabulary Builder Lessons.

The key to doing well on vocabulary tests is to increase and enrich your vocabulary as much as possible prior to taking the test. But if you don't recognize a word, you can use the following reasoning technique to try to determine the meaning of the term:

1. What do I hear when I repeat the word to myself?
2. Does it resemble any words I know?
3. Does it include any familiar roots, prefixes, or suffixes? (You will find a list of these below.)
4. Do the multiple-choice answers give me any clue?

Finally, try to relax and be confident. Most people know more words than they think they do.

ROOTS

Root	Meaning	Root	Meaning
1. *anglo*	English, Great Britain	11. *manu*	hand
2. *anthrop*	humankind, people	12. *morph*	form
3. *bibl*	book	13. *omni*	all
4. *bio*	life	14. *phil*	love, lover
5. *carn*	meat	15. *porc*	pig
6. *chron*	time	16. *reg*	king, ruler
7. *culp*	blame	17. *sang*	blood
8. *geo*	earth	18. *scribe*	write
9. *graph*	write	19. *theo*	God, belief in God
10. *herb*	plant, vegetable	20. *vor*	eat, devour

PREFIXES

Prefix	Meaning	Prefix	Meaning
1. *a-*	without, from	6. *post-*	after
2. *circum-*	around	7. *pre-*	before
3. *ex-*	away from, out	8. *semi-*	half
4. *mono-*	one	9. *syn-*	together, with
5. *poly-*	many	10. *tri-*	three

SUFFIXES

Suffix	Meaning	Suffix	Meaning
1. *-able*	able, likely	5. *-ism*	act, doctrine
2. *-ate*	cause, make	6. *-ist*	one who
3. *-cide*	killing of	7. *-logy*	study of
4. *-ine*	of, relating to	8. *-ous*	having, possessing

Part One

Directions: Select the word or term that does not belong.

1. a. adroit
   b. coordinated
   c. skillful
   d. agile
   e. awkward

2. a. esoteric
   b. obvious
   c. widely known
   d. well publicized
   e. ordinary

3. a. periphery
   b. edge
   c. core
   d. outside
   e. outer reaches

4. a. true
   b. specious
   c. valid
   d. well-reasoned
   e. provable

5. a. synthesize
   b. blend
   c. join
   d. fracture
   e. merge

6. a. upbraid
   b. scold
   c. praise
   d. criticize
   e. attack

Part Two

Directions: Select the word that is most nearly *opposite* to the boldface word.

1. **ameliorate**
   a. improve
   b. worsen
   c. exaggerate
   d. lose
   e. cheat

2. **credulous**
   a. fetching
   b. approving
   c. gullible
   d. skeptical
   e. repellant

3. **malign**
   a. insult
   b. tease
   c. praise
   d. wander
   e. preside

4. **sagacity**
   a. ignorance
   b. wisdom
   c. tolerance
   d. laziness
   e. concern

5. **stolid**
   a. weird
   b. hardworking
   c. gifted
   d. praiseworthy
   e. emotional

6. **verbosity**
   a. cooperation
   b. silence
   c. earnestness
   d. vigor
   e. dishonesty

Part Three

Directions: Select the word pair that has the same relationship as the boldface pair.

1. **ascetic : pleasure**
   a. teacher : rugged
   b. scientist : superstition
   c. wanderer : forests
   d. comedian : applause
   e. astrologer : books

2. **miracle : benumb**
   a. tragedy : horrify
   b. sporting event : gratify
   c. modern art : edify
   d. feast : repel
   e. college education : glorify

3. **despot : subjects**
   a. chef : patrons
   b. officer : civilians
   c. coach : players
   d. teacher : administrators
   e. banker : customers

4. **perfunctory : enthusiastic**
   a. overt : deceptive
   b. treacherous : deceitful
   c. apologetic : cautious
   d. slovenly : inert
   e. credible : critical

5. **oracle : truth**
   a. restaurant : privacy
   b. resort : recreation
   c. slum : pleasure
   d. store : fashion
   e. church : adulation

6. **sycophant : flattery**
   a. quarterback : courage
   b. butcher : meat
   c. liar : deception
   d. poet : morality
   e. mechanic : pleasure

Part Four

Directions: Select the word that correctly completes the sentence.

1. The conversation was so _____ that Jonathan fell asleep.
   a. ephemeral
   b. empirical
   c. peripheral
   d. voracious
   e. banal

2. Hermione tried to _____ her mother into letting her stay home from school.
   a. ameliorate
   b. cajole
   c. foment
   d. mollify
   e. upbraid

3. Rather than lasting forever, Joe and Patsy's love proved _____ .
   a. ephemeral
   b. credulous
   c. sardonic
   d. mendacious
   e. verbose

4. Government agents suspected him of _____ but could not prove he was actually trying to start a revolution.
   a. ascetism
   b. chauvinism
   c. sedition
   d. philanthropy
   e. verbosity

5. Rodney used to be _____ , but lately he has become much more approachable.
   a. blasphemous
   b. supercilious
   c. circumspect
   d. stolid
   e. sinuous

6. He has a(n) _____ appetite for basketball. Last week he watched seven games on TV.
   a. voracious
   b. culpable
   c. impious
   d. specious
   e. covert

Part Five

Directions: Read each word pair and determine whether the words are synonyms or antonyms. Write *s* if the words in the pair are synonyms. Write *a* if the words in the pair are antonyms.

1. blasé–bored
2. amorphous–defined
3. charlatan–fraud
4. foment–discourage
5. pragmatic–idealistic
6. sardonic–sarcastic

Part Six

Directions: Select the word(s) that best complete(s) the sentence.

1. It's usually considered highly blasphemous to ridicule someone else's _____ .
   a. pet
   b. past
   c. religion
   d. reading habits
   e. food

2. A philanthropist would be described as _____ .
   a. selfish
   b. petty
   c. indulgent
   d. generous
   e. impulsive

3. A pedantic teacher would ask questions that were exceedingly _____ .
   a. humorous
   b. obscure
   c. obvious
   d. juvenile
   e. popular

4. An empiricist would probably reject information acquired from a(n) _____ .
   a. geologist
   b. biologist
   c. anthropologist
   d. geneticist
   e. astrologer

5. A sardonic individual should expect to make _____ .
   a. friends
   b. enemies
   c. money
   d. inventions
   e. mistakes

6. An iconoclast would challenge what many people consider _____ .
   a. sacred
   b. material
   c. ugly
   d. trivial
   e. frivolous

Part Seven

Directions: Match the magazine article title with the word most closely associated with the subject of the article.

1.	candor	a.	"A Photo Essay of Snakes"
2.	culpable	b.	"Being Honest With Yourself and Others"
3.	fallacious	c.	"How Good Luck Changed My Life"
4.	esoteric	d.	"Seven Logical Mistakes"
5.	sinuous	e.	"Heidegger, Dilthey, and the Crisis of Historicism"
6.	fortuitous	f.	"Who's Really Responsible for Teenage Crime?"

ADDITIONAL LISTS

Each word in the following lists has been included in the vocabulary portion of a recent SAT examination. Try to learn the words that are unfamiliar. These are useful vocabulary terms that appear frequently in newspaper and journal articles.

Vocabulary List 1

1. acerbity — sourness of character
2. aphorism — wise saying
3. austere — severe
4. broach — bring up
5. circumvent — get around
6. complacent — self-satisfied
7. contumacious — disobedient
8. covenant — agreement
9. dolorous — distressing, painful
10. duress — pressure, stress
11. extraneous — not essential, irrelevant
12. extricate — disentangle
13. finical — fussy
14. foment — stir up
15. fortuitous — accidental
16. hiatus — pause, gap
17. immutable — unchangeable
18. impugn — question the honesty of
19. insidious — sly
20. lucent — bright, clear
21. malign — slander
22. misanthrope — hater of people
23. nefarious — wicked
24. nocturnal — active at night
25. nurture — feed, nourish
26. overt — open
27. perspicacity — quick understanding
28. pique — resentment
29. predatory — plundering, destroying
30. predilection — preference
31. pundit — authority, expert
32. rationalize — to excuse, justify
33. recumbent — reclining, reposing
34. risible — laughable
35. sanguine — hopeful
36. sedulous — diligent, hard-working
37. specious — deceptive
38. unmitigated — absolute, complete
39. vertex — height, apex
40. visage — appearance, facial expression

Vocabulary List 2

1. acquiesce — agree
2. altercation — quarrel
3. cavil — to find fault
4. compunction — remorse
5. copious — abundant
6. covert — secret
7. demure — modest
8. dormant — inactive
9. efficacy — effectiveness
10. emulate — imitate
11. entreaty — a plea
12. equivocate — lie cleverly
13. flagitious — vicious
14. impecunious — penniless
15. inadvertent — unintentional
16. indigent — poverty-stricken
17. iniquitous — evil
18. inveterate — deep-seated, habitual
19. languid — dull, limp
20. machination — plot, scheme
21. mollify — appease, calm
22. neophyte — newcomer
23. noisome — offensive
24. obtuse — stupid, slow
25. opprobrious — shameful
26. parody — humorous imitation
27. peruse — to read with care
28. pithy — concise
29. preponderate — predominate
30. quandary — an uncertainty, confusion
31. recant — renounce former beliefs
32. ribald — vulgar
33. sapient — wise
34. sinuous — winding
35. splenetic — irritable
36. succor — assistance
37. truncate — shorten
38. upbraid — scold
39. vicissitude — a change
40. vociferous — loud

Vocabulary List 3

1. abhor   hate
2. acme   highest point
3. affluence   riches
4. amnesty   pardon for offenses against a government
5. assuage   lessen
6. bilious   bad-tempered
7. blasé   bored
8. circumspect   cautious
9. contraband   smuggled goods
10. deleterious   harmful
11. despot   dictator
12. dissident   disagreeing
13. erudite   scholarly
14. felicitous   appropriate
15. garrulous   talkative
16. gesticulate   make gestures
17. hue   shade (of color)
18. impasse   standstill
19. ineluctable   unavoidable
20. intransigent   stubborn
21. ken   field of knowledge
22. lucid   clear
23. malinger   to fake illness or injury to avoid work
24. mnemonic   assisting memory
25. myriad   very numerous
26. narcissistic   self-centered
27. odious   hateful
28. palpitate   beat quickly
29. paraphrase   restate
30. pedant   intellectual snob
31. pragmatic   practical
32. promiscuous   lacking standards of selection
33. recalcitrant   resisting authority, habitually disobedient
34. restive   nervous
35. sardonic   sarcastic
36. stolid   unemotional
37. sybarite   lover of luxury
38. tirade   outburst
39. vagary   whim
40. vitiated   contaminated, weakened

Vocabulary List 4

1. adamant — unyielding
2. anomaly — something irregular or abnormal
3. antipathy — hatred for
4. apathy — lack of feeling
5. assiduous — persistent
6. autonomous — self-governing
7. banal — trite, commonplace
8. candor — open honesty
9. caprice — a whim
10. castigate — severely criticize
11. chicanery — trickery
12. depraved — morally corrupt
13. dissonance — discord, harsh sounds
14. dour — gloomy
15. ebullient — full of enthusiasm
16. ecstatic — overpowered with delight
17. enervate — weaken
18. engender — cause, bring about
19. ephemeral — short-lived
20. esoteric — understood by only a few
21. fiasco — complete, utter failure
22. flaccid — limp
23. laconic — using few words
24. latent — unrevealed, hidden
25. lethargic — sluggish
26. lugubrious — ridiculously sorrowful
27. moribund — dying
28. parsimonious — excessively frugal
29. perfidious — traitorous
30. perfunctory — indifferent
31. polemic — controversial argument
32. procrastinate — put off
33. prototype — model
34. regressive — going backward
35. sagacity — wisdom
36. tacit — unexpressed but understood
37. tenuous — unsubstantial
38. ubiquitous — everywhere at the same time
39. vapid — dull
40. voluptuous — sensual

Vocabulary List 5

1.	adroit	clever
2.	animosity	hostility
3.	apposite	appropriate
4.	bourgeois	middle class
5.	cerebration	use of reason
6.	coadjutor	assistant
7.	concomitant	accompanying
8.	corroboration	confirmation
9.	culpable	blamable
10.	dichotomy	division into two parts
11.	dotage	feeble old age
12.	enigma	puzzle, mystery
13.	fecundity	productiveness
14.	flamboyant	showy
15.	forte	strong point
16.	gamut	range
17.	impetus	energy of motion, force
18.	inchoate	just beginning
19.	indolence	laziness
20.	innocuous	harmless
21.	invidious	offensive
22.	licentious	immoral
23.	maimed	crippled, mutilated
24.	meretricious	flashy, false
25.	nadir	low point
26.	nexus	link
27.	nonentity	person of no influence
28.	obviate	prevent
29.	opulent	luxurious
30.	paucity	insufficiency
31.	petulant	bad-tempered
32.	placid	calm
33.	profligate	wasteful
34.	recondite	ambiguous
35.	retinue	attentive group
36.	salient	noticeable
37.	saturnine	morose, gloomy
38.	spurious	false
39.	succulent	juicy
40.	turbid	muddy

Vocabulary List 6

1.	affinity	mutual attraction
2.	amalgamate	join
3.	apex	high point
4.	aspersion	slander
5.	chimerical	absurdly improbable
6.	coalesce	merge
7.	cogitate	think hard
8.	coterie	social group
9.	debauch	corrupt
10.	diurnal	daily
11.	ductile	easily swayed, flexible
12.	exiguous	meager
13.	fetish	obsession
14.	foible	weakness
15.	imbroglio	tangled confusion
16.	impolitic	unwise
17.	incipient	beginning
18.	ingenuous	innocently frank
19.	innuendo	sly hint
20.	irascible	easily angered
21.	limpid	clear, transparent
22.	malevolent	spiteful, evil
23.	nuance	subtle variation
24.	periphery	edge, perimeter
25.	piquant	stimulating
26.	plethoric	full, abundant
27.	prognosticate	predict
28.	pulchritude	beauty
29.	reconnoiter	spy out
30.	reprobation	disapproval
31.	salubrious	health-giving
32.	schism	division
33.	somnolent	drowsy
34.	stratagem	trick
35.	supplication	prayer
36.	umbrage	resentment
37.	vacuity	emptiness
38.	virile	manly, masculine
39.	voracious	all-devouring, greedy
40.	xenophobic	fearful of foreigners

Vocabulary List 7

1. abstruse — difficult to understand
2. acrid — biting, harsh
3. affront — insult
4. anachronism — error in chronology
5. august — impressive
6. cacophony — noise, harsh sounds
7. chagrin — embarrassment
8. clandestine — secret
9. desultory — occasional
10. eclectic — gathered from many sources
11. egregious — extremely bad
12. enamored — fond of
13. eschew — stay away from
14. facile — easy
15. fickle — unstable
16. generic — common
17. harbinger — sign, omen
18. hypochondria — imagined ill health
19. ineptitude — clumsiness
20. intrepid — brave
21. juxtapose — set together
22. labyrinth — confusing pattern, maze
23. Machiavellian — deceitful
24. nomad — wanderer
25. ostentatious — showy
26. pensive — meditative, thoughtful
27. philistine — uncultured
28. poignant — biting, painful
29. prate — chatter
30. redress — repay, make amends
31. reticent — reluctant (to speak)
32. satiated — full
33. staccato — cut short, disconnected
34. succinct — concise
35. sycophant — flatterer
36. tyro — beginner
37. verbosity — wordiness
38. virtuoso — accomplished performer
39. vivacity — liveliness
40. wanton — reckless

Grammar and Usage

INTRODUCTION

Tests that measure your knowledge of the rules of English are an unavoidable reality. The ACT, the SAT II, the GED, and many individual college placement examinations include sections addressing English usage.

In short, these tests measure your knowledge of the rules of English grammar. It's true that reviewing these rules will help you improve your performance on the tests, but there are other rewards as well. In speaking and writing every day, you demonstrate your knowledge of grammar and usage. Making a good impression both socially and at work depends upon a solid understanding of standard English. Once you have gained that, it will be easier to focus on the communication itself, without the distraction of guessing about proper punctuation or verb tense.

You will begin your review with an overview of general usage rules. Next, you can focus on the variations of these rules. In the process you probably will discover that you know more than you thought you did. You can approach the test with confidence in your ability to do well.

TEN BASIC RULES OF ENGLISH USAGE

Begin your review by memorizing the following ten rules.

1. **Use complete sentences; avoid fragments and run-ons.**

   incorrect: Knowing the territory. Juan moved ahead.
   correct: Knowing the territory, Juan moved ahead.

   incorrect: Mabel cooked the dinner, Juan jogged around the block.
   correct: Mabel cooked the dinner. Juan jogged around the block.

2. **Make subjects and verbs agree in number.**

   incorrect: One of the girls <u>have</u> left town.
   correct: One of the girls <u>has</u> left town.

3. **Make pronouns agree with their antecedents.**

   incorrect: The club decided to expel <u>their</u> irresponsible members.
   correct: The club decided to expel <u>its</u> irresponsible members.

4. **Use the correct case of personal pronouns.**

   incorrect: He gave the job to Barney and <u>I</u>.
   correct: He gave the job to Barney and <u>me</u>.

5. **Use the correct form of verbs.**

   incorrect: Lucy's chatter <u>has began</u> to irritate me.
   correct: Lucy's chatter <u>has begun</u> to irritate me.

6. **Use adjectives and adverbs correctly.**

   incorrect: The young dog moved <u>awkward</u>.
   correct: The young dog moved <u>awkwardly</u>.

7. **Construct equal elements of a sentence in parallel form.**

   incorrect: Mary Jane enjoys sailing, reading, and <u>to play</u> golf.
   correct: Mary Jane enjoys sailing, reading, and <u>playing</u> golf.

8. **Do not confuse words that are similar in spelling or pronunciation.**

   incorrect: Actions speak louder <u>then</u> words.
   correct: Actions speak louder <u>than</u> words.

9. **Capitalize correctly.**

   incorrect: Harriet does not like to camp in the <u>Summer</u>.
   correct: Harriet does not like to camp in the <u>summer</u>.

10. **Punctuate correctly.**

   incorrect: <u>Jack Jill and Steve</u> went to the store.
   correct: <u>Jack, Jill, and Steve</u> went to the store.

Now turn to page 60 to study the variations of each rule.

VARIATIONS ON THE TEN BASIC RULES

1. **Use complete sentences; avoid fragments and run-ons.**

   a. A fragment can be corrected by changing an inappropriate verb or adding a missing verb.

      | incorrect: | Sue <u>running</u> to the bakery. |
      | correct: | Sue <u>was running</u> to the bakery. |
      | or: | Sue <u>ran</u> to the bakery. |

   b. A fragment can be corrected by adding a missing subject.

      | incorrect: | Was governing with dignity. |
      | correct: | <u>The old leader</u> was governing with dignity. |

   c. A fragment can be corrected by adding a missing subject and verb.

      | incorrect: | To go on vacation tomorrow. |
      | correct: | <u>Steve decided</u> to go on vacation tomorrow. |

   d. A run-on can be eliminated by adding a period and capital letter appropriately.

      | incorrect: | Marcia plays beautifully, the audience cheers. |
      | correct: | Marcia plays beautifully. The audience cheers. |

   e. A run-on can be eliminated by adding a semicolon.

      | incorrect: | Marcia plays beautifully, the audience cheers. |
      | correct: | Marcia plays beautifully; the audience cheers. |

   f. A run-on can be eliminated by adding a subordinating conjunction.

      | incorrect: | Marcia plays beautifully, the audience cheers. |
      | correct: | <u>When</u> Marcia plays beautifully, the audience cheers. |

2. **Make subjects and verbs agree in number.**

   a. A singular subject always requires a singular verb, even when the subject is followed by a preposition with a plural object.

incorrect: Each of the horses <u>are</u> running in the race.

correct: Each of the horses <u>is</u> running in the race.

b.   The following words as subjects always require a singular verb: *each, either, neither, one, everyone, every one, no one, anyone, someone, everybody, nobody, anybody, somebody.*

incorrect: Neither of the teachers <u>are</u> in a hurry.

correct: Neither of the teachers <u>is</u> in a hurry.

c.   The following words as subjects always require plural verbs: *few, both, many, several.*

incorrect: Many of us <u>was</u> surprised by the speech.

correct: Many of us <u>were</u> surprised by the speech.

d.   The following words as subjects require singular or plural verbs, depending upon the meaning of the sentence: *some, any, all, none, most.*

incorrect: Some of the players <u>was</u> tired.

correct: Some of the players <u>were</u> less tired.

incorrect: Some of the steak <u>were</u> eaten.

correct: Some of the steak <u>was</u> eaten.

3. **Make pronouns agree with their antecedents.**

a.   A pronoun must agree in number (singular or plural) with its antecedent, the noun or pronoun to which it refers.

incorrect: One of the singers smiles during <u>their</u> solo.

correct: One of the singers smiles during <u>her</u> solo.

or: One of the singers smiles during <u>his</u> solo.

b.   A pronoun must have a clear antecedent, a noun or pronoun to which it refers.

incorrect: The gentleman asked the waiter to bring <u>it</u>.

correct: The gentleman asked the waiter to bring <u>a glass</u>.

4. **Use the correct case of personal pronouns.**

   a. The subject form (<u>I, he, she, we, they</u>) must be used when the pronoun is the subject of a verb.

      incorrect: <u>Her</u> has a new car.
      correct: <u>She</u> has a new car.

   b. The subject form must be used when the pronoun follows a form of the word *be*.

      incorrect: It is <u>me</u>.
      correct: It is <u>I</u>.

   c. The object form (*me, him, her, us, them*) must be used when the pronoun is the object of an action verb.

      incorrect: I saw <u>they</u> at the concert.
      correct: I saw <u>them</u> at the concert.

   d. The object form must be used when the pronoun is the object of a preposition.

      incorrect: He gave the water to Wally and <u>I</u>.
      correct: He gave the water to Wally and <u>me</u>.

   e. The object form must be used when the pronoun is the object of an infinitive.

      incorrect: To teach <u>they</u>, you will need patience.
      correct: To teach <u>them</u>, you will need patience.

   f. The object form must be used when the pronoun is the object of a participle.

      incorrect: There goes Bill chasing <u>she</u>.
      correct: There goes Bill chasing <u>her</u>.

5. **Use the correct form of verbs.**

Regular English verbs form both their past and past participle tenses by adding *-d* or *-ed* to the infinitive forms. Many English verbs, however, have irregular forms. Learn the correct forms of the following commonly used irregular verbs.

INFINITIVE	PAST	PAST PARTICIPLE
1. bear	bore	have borne
2. beat	beat	have beaten
3. bring	brought	have brought
4. choose	chose	have chosen

5.	drive	drove	have driven
6.	drink	drank	have drunk
7.	fling	flung	have flung
8.	go	went	have gone
9.	lay	laid	have laid
10.	lie	lay	have lain
11.	ring	rang	have rung
12.	rise	rose	have risen
13.	set	set	have set
14.	shake	shook	have shaken
15.	shine	shone or shined	have shone or have shined
16.	sing	sang or sung	have sung
17.	sink	sank or sunk	have sunk
18.	swim	swam	have swum
19.	swing	swung	have swung
20.	tear	tore	have torn

6. **Use adjectives and adverbs correctly.**

    a.   Adverbs modify action verbs, adjectives, or other adverbs.

          incorrect: Sam hits the ball <u>bad</u>.
          correct: Sam hits the ball <u>badly</u>.

    b.   Adjectives, rather than adverbs, follow linking (nonaction) verbs.

          incorrect: That banana smells <u>badly</u>.
          correct: That banana smells <u>bad</u>.

    c.   The comparative form (*larger, funnier,* etc.) of the adjective is used to compare two things.

          incorrect: William is the <u>biggest</u> of the two boys.
          correct: William is the <u>bigger</u> of the two boys.

    d.   The superlative form (*largest, funniest,* etc.) of the adjective is used to compare three or more things.

          incorrect: Of Brooks, Allen, or Leno, who is the <u>funnier</u> comedian?
          correct: Of Brooks, Allen, or Leno, who is the <u>funniest</u> comedian?

7. **Construct equal elements of a sentence in parallel form.**

   a. The same kind of word construction should be used in any series of phrases.

      | incorrect: | Painting, gardening, and <u>to cook</u> are Jill's favorite activities. |
      | correct: | Painting, gardening, and <u>cooking</u> are Jill's favorite activities. |

   b. Linking verbs require parallel word forms.

      | incorrect: | To earn is better than <u>begging</u>. |
      | correct: | To earn is better than <u>to beg</u>. |
      | or: | Earning is better than <u>begging</u>. |

8. **Do not confuse words that are similar in spelling or pronunciation.**

   a. *accept* and *except*

      I can't <u>accept</u> (admit to) the notion that only men can be soldiers.

      Everyone went to the supper <u>except</u> (but) Paul.

   b. *affect* and *effect*

      Bobby was deeply <u>affected</u> (influenced) by his older brother's speech.

      What was the <u>effect</u> (result) of the flood in Youngstown?

   c. *allude* and *elude*

      He was not angry, but he did <u>allude</u> (refer indirectly) to the fact that I had lost the key.

      The quarterback <u>eluded</u> (evaded) three tacklers before completing the pass.

   d. *allusion* and *illusion*

      During her cross-examination, the prosecutor made several <u>allusions</u> (indirect references) to the suspicious behavior of the defendant.

      Are you still under the <u>illusion</u> (false impression) that candy bars are good for you?

   e. *already* and *all ready*

      Sybil had <u>already</u> (by this time) returned from Ireland when the airline strike began.

Are you <u>all ready</u> (completely prepared) to go to the concert?

f. *altogether* and *all together*

The judge was not <u>altogether</u> (entirely) convinced by the defendant's testimony.

Are the members of the group <u>all together</u> (everyone gathered)?

g. *complement* and *compliment*

Peanut butter and jelly are the perfect <u>complements</u> (elements that make a whole).

The chef gracefully accepted our <u>compliments</u> (expressions of praise) about his peanut butter sandwich.

h. *discreet* and *discrete*

It was not <u>discreet</u> (prudent) of the senator to question the honesty of the president.

The directions clearly identified the <u>discrete</u> (separate) parts of the process.

i. *disinterested* and *uninterested*

The arbitrator was a <u>disinterested</u> (impartial) participant in the negotiations.

The crowd was <u>uninterested</u> in (indifferent to) the outcome of the trial.

j. *farther* and *further*

George can run <u>farther</u> (distance) than Reggie can.

The <u>further</u> (time) we discussed the issue, the angrier we became.

k. *healthful* and *healthy*

The campers looked <u>healthy</u> (having good health) after all that fresh air and exercise.

It has been said that Minnesota has a <u>healthful</u> (causing good health) climate.

l. *imply* and *infer*

Without actually saying so, the waiter <u>implied</u> (suggested) that I might prefer a different entree.

I <u>inferred</u> (concluded) from his happy expression that he had not been given a homework assignment.

m. *nauseated* and *nauseous*

He became <u>nauseated</u> (to feel nausea) after consuming the spoiled milk.

He was almost overcome by the <u>nauseous</u> (causing nausea, disgusting) stench of the spoiled meat.

n. *respectfully* and *respectively*

When Wanda learns to treat people <u>respectfully</u> (with respect), she will make more friends.

Star Wars, Superman II, and *La Strada* were directed by Lucas, Lester, and Fellini <u>respectively</u> (singly in order).

o. *stationary* and *stationery*

The soldiers stood in a <u>stationary</u> (not moving) position for four hours.

Julie borrowed the <u>stationery</u> (writing paper and supplies) from Zelda.

p. *tortuous* and *torturous*

The road to the cabin was quite <u>tortuous</u> (winding).

The seven-hour workout in the ninety-degree heat was <u>torturous</u> (very painful).

9. **Capitalize correctly.**

Although there are many rules of capitalization, many capitalization questions on tests are based on three variations.

a. Seasons of the year never are capitalized.

incorrect: I love to swim in <u>Winter.</u>
correct: I love to swim in <u>winter.</u>

b. Directions are capitalized only when they are used to designate a part of the country.

incorrect: He grew up in the <u>southwest.</u>
correct: He grew up in the <u>Southwest.</u>

incorrect: Drive <u>Southwest</u> to get to the auction.
correct: Drive <u>southwest</u> to get to the auction.

c. Words such as *mother, coach,* and *president* are capitalized only when they are used as titles for people.

incorrect: I told the <u>Coach</u> that my <u>Mother</u> likes <u>president</u> Gleason.
correct: I told the <u>coach</u> that my <u>mother</u> likes <u>President</u> Gleason.

incorrect: I asked <u>mother</u> to meet <u>coach</u> Carver to discuss the <u>President's</u> politics.

correct: I asked <u>Mother</u> to meet <u>Coach</u> Carver to discuss the <u>president's</u> politics.

10. **Punctuate correctly.**

Many of the punctuation questions on standardized tests concern the use of commas.

    a. Commas should be used to separate items in a series.

        incorrect: Charles James William and Digger lost in the tournament.

        correct: Charles, James, William, and Digger lost in the tournament.

    b. A comma should be used to set off a long introductory phrase in a sentence.

        incorrect: Relaxing in the cool shade and sipping fresh lemonade Sam suddenly remembered that his car was running.

        correct: Relaxing in the cool shade and sipping fresh lemonade, Sam suddenly remembered that his car was running.

    c. A comma should be used to set off an adverbial clause at the beginning of a sentence from the rest of the sentence.

        incorrect: After the rain stopped we went to the beach.

        correct: After the rain stopped, we went to the beach.

    d. A comma should be used to separate two independent clauses joined by a coordinating conjunction (*and, or, but,* etc.).

        incorrect: The boy fell down but his mother did not notice.

        correct: The boy fell down, but his mother did not notice.

SAMPLE EXERCISES

To check your understanding of the ten basic rules of English usage and their variations, complete the following sample exercises.

Exercise 1

Find the mistake in each of the following sentences and rewrite the sentence correctly. Then write the number and text of the basic rule that pertains to that mistake. Each sentence includes only one rule violation. No rule violation appears more than once in the set of ten sentences.

1. Before examinations, George does not eat good.

   Rewrite:

   Rule No.:

2. Bill's brother a huge man used to play professional football.

   Rewrite:

   Rule No.:

3. Lay down on the ground, Bowser, so that I can clean your paws.

   Rewrite:

   Rule No.:

4. Neither of the girls are fond of pizza.

   Rewrite:

   Rule No.:

5. Are the ladies and gentlemen at that table already to order?

   Rewrite:

   Rule No.:

6. Every one of the men spent several hours working in their own garden.

   Rewrite:

   Rule No.:

7. Mr. Bolivar prefers to read, to exercise, and piano playing.

   Rewrite:

   Rule No.:

8. Many people living in the south like to eat grits.

   Rewrite:

   Rule No.:

9. The elderly woman gave the ice cream to Dorothy and I.

   Rewrite:

   Rule No.:

10. While Bob was away. The cat ran off with his slippers.

    Rewrite:

    Rule No.:

Exercise 2

Find the mistake in each of the following sentences and rewrite the sentence correctly. Then write the number and text of the basic rule that pertains to that mistake. Each sentence includes only one rule violation. No rule violation appears more than once in the set of ten sentences.

1. Meagan plays regular with the Baldino children.

   Rewrite:

   Rule No.:

2. Letitia's favorite season of the year is Spring.

   Rewrite:

   Rule No.:

3. The booster club held an election to select their officers.

   Rewrite:

   Rule No:

4. Both of the golfers has had a low score.

   Rewrite:

   Rule No.:

5. According to many campers, rafting is better than to canoe.

   Rewrite:

   Rule No.:

6. Vijay enjoys the great outdoors, Helen prefers libraries and bookstores.

   Rewrite:

   Rule No.:

7. It was me whose poor play cost us the game.

   Rewrite:

   Rule No.:

8. Shouting and stamping his feet the toddler refused to get ready for bed.

   Rewrite:

   Rule No.:

9. After high school, Derek lead a solitary life.

   Rewrite:

   Rule No.:

10. Rowena has trouble accepting complements.

    Rewrite:

    Rule No.:

PRACTICE TESTS

The following standard English tests use a format similar to that used on the ACT, the GED, and several standardized English tests. This format requires you to apply your knowledge of the rules of English to entire paragraphs instead of single sentences. This is more challenging, but it also permits a more reliable measure of your understanding of proper usage. Further, it is typical of the process you should follow when proofreading your own writing.

Thus, these Practice Tests do more than prepare you to perform well on achievement tests. You will be mastering skills you can apply throughout life.

Pressure

(1) Pressure often results from the fear of failing what people think they should acheive. (2) If the chances for success are slim, people do not worry about failure. (3) But if they suspect that success is possible, they begin to worry. (4) Such anxiety can occur before students take a test in school. (5) Athletes might experience pressure participating in a sport in which they have already demonstrated talent. (6) If businesspeople come up with feasible ideas, they are apt to worry more than if they come up with impractical one's. (7) And the tension job applicants experience before a job interview grows the more that they suspect the job is within their reach. (8) If people except this pressure as both inevitable and desirable, they will be able to handle it better. (9) Such self-awareness will tell them that nothing is wrong. (10) Indeed, this feeling of pressure means that individuals have set certain high standards for themselves. (11) In other words, a feeling of pressure can drive people forward to reach new goles. (12) Yet, if people worry too much about pressure, they can inhibit there freedom. (13) Then they have lost their ability to improve themselves?

1. Sentence 1: Pressure often results from the fear of failing what people think they should acheive.

    What correction should be made to this sentence?

    (a) change *think* to *had thought*
    (b) change the spelling of *acheive* to *achieve*
    (c) remove *from*
    (d) move *often* to the end of the sentence
    (e) no change is required

2. Sentences 2 and 3: If the chances for success are slim, people do not worry about failure. But if they suspect that success is possible, they begin to worry.

    The most effective combination of Sentences 2 and 3 would include which of the following groups of words?

    (a) worry about failure, but if
    (b) worry about failure but if
    (c) worry about failure and if
    (d) worry about failure, and if
    (e) worry about failure, so if

3. Sentence 4: Such anxiety can occur before students take a test in school.

    What correction should be made to this sentence?

    (a) change the spelling of *anxiety* to *anxeity*
    (b) change *can occur* to *occurring*
    (c) replace *before* with *be for*
    (d) place a comma after *occur*
    (e) no change is required

4. Sentence 6: If businesspeople come up with feasible ideas, they are apt to worry more than if they come up with *impractical one's.*

    Which of the following is the best way to write the italicized portion of this sentence? If you think the original is the best way, choose Option (a).

    (a) impractical one's.
    (b) immpractical one's.
    (c) impractical ones.
    (d) impractical ones'.
    (e) impracticle one's.

5. Sentence 8: If people except this pressure as both inevitable and desirable, they will be able to handle it better.

    What correction should be made to this sentence?

    (a) remove the comma after *desirable*
    (b) place a comma after *inevitable*
    (c) change *except* to *accept*
    (d) change the spelling of *handle* to *handel*
    (e) no change is required

6. Sentence 10: Indeed, this feeling of pressure means that individuals have set certain high standards for themselves.

    What correction should be made to this sentence?

    (a) remove the comma after *Indeed*
    (b) change *means* to *mean*
    (c) replace *feeling* with *feelings*
    (d) change *themselves* to *itself*
    (e) no change is required

7. Sentence 11: In other words, a feeling of pressure can drive people forward to reach new goles.

    What correction should be made to this sentence?

    (a) change the spelling of *goles* to *goals*
    (b) change the spelling of *pressure* to *presure*
    (c) change *people* to *you*
    (d) replace *drive* with *drove*
    (e) no change is required

8. Sentence 12: Yet, if people worry too much about pressure, *they can inhibit there* freedom.

    Which of the following is the best way to write the italicized portion of the sentence? If you think the original is the best way, choose Option (a).

    (a) they can inhibit there
    (b) they can inhibit their
    (c) they can inhibit they're
    (d) he can inhibit his
    (e) they can inhibits there

9. Sentence 13: Then they have lost their ability to improve themselves?

    What correction should be made to this sentence?

    (a) replace *Then* with *If*
    (b) change *have* to *has*
    (c) replace the question mark at the end of the sentence with a period
    (d) change the spelling of *ability* to *abilitie*
    (e) no change is required

Reading

(1) Comprehending difficult reading material is no simple task. (2) One can, however, follow a system to make the task less imposing, whether you are reading a chapter from a textbook or a serious article in a magazine. (3) Surprisingly, the first thing to remember is not to read immediately. (4) If you barge into a passage unprepared, you will almost certainly confuse yourself. (5) Instead, grasp an overal sense of the subject by skimming the material first. (6) To skim, study the title the subtitle, the topic sentences, and any italicized words. (7) After you have successfully skimmed, you should know the topic of the article and understand the point the author is making about that topic. (8) After you have skimmed, write down the significant questions that the article should answer. (9) Finally, when you actually read the article, underline portions that answer *your* questions. (10) Also, underline any other passages that captures your attention. (11) After you completed your first reading, write down the answers to your questions plus the answers to any other questions the article posed. (12) Finally, reread the article one last time, looking for any points you might have missed the first time through. (13) Before you put the article away, write a quick summary, making sure to include the answers to all of your questions. (14) While this method consumes quite a bit of time initially, it saves time later on. (15) Try it.

1. Sentence 2: *One can, however, follow a system to make* the task less imposing, whether you are reading a chapter from a textbook or a serious article in a magazine.

   Which of the following is the best way to write the italicized part of this sentence? If you think the original is the best way, choose Option (a).

   (a) One can, however, follow a system to make
   (b) You can, however, follow a system to make
   (c) And you can follow a system to make
   (d) And one can follow a system to make
   (e) But one can follow a system making

2. Sentences 3 and 4: Surprisingly, the first thing to remember is not to read immediately. If you barge into a passage unprepared, you will almost certainly confuse yourself.

The most effective combination of Sentences 3 and 4 would include which of the following groups of words?

(a) because if you
(b) even though
(c) preparing to
(d) confusing yourself
(e) remembering the passage

3. Sentence 5: *Instead, grasp an overal sense* of the subject by skimming the material first.

Which of the following is the best way to write the italicized portion of this sentence? If you think the original is the best way, choose Option (a).

(a) Instead, grasp an overal sense
(b) Instead grasp an overal sense
(c) Instead, grasp an overall sense
(d) Indeed, grasp an overall sense
(e) Instead, grasp an overal sence

4. Sentence 6: To skim, study the title the subtitle, the topic sentences, and any italicized words.

What correction should be made to this sentence?

(a) insert a comma after *title*
(b) remove the comma after *subtitle*
(c) change *topic sentences* to *topic-sentences*
(d) change the spelling of *italicized* to *italisized*
(e) no change is required

5. Sentence 8: After you have skimmed, write down the significant questions that the article should answer.

What correction should be made to this sentence?

(a) remove the comma after *skimmed*
(b) change the spelling of *skimmed* to *skimed*
(c) replace *significant* with *significantly*
(d) change *should answer* to *has answered*
(e) no change is required

6. Sentence 10: Also, underline any other passages that captures your attention.

What correction should be made to this sentence?

(a)   change *captures* to *capture*
(b)   remove the comma after *Also*
(c)   replace *underline* with *under line*
(d)   change the spelling of *passages* to *pasages*
(e)   no change is required

7.   Sentence 11: After you completed your first reading, write down the answers to your questions plus the answers to any other questions the article posed.

What correction should be made to this sentence?

(a)   remove the comma after *reading*
(b)   change *completed* to *has completed*
(c)   change *completed* to *have completed*
(d)   replace *your* with *you're*
(e)   no change is required

8.   Sentence 12: Finally, reread the article one last time, looking for any points you might have missed the first time through.

What correction should be made to this sentence?

(a)   change the spelling of *Finally* to *Finaly*
(b)   replace the comma after *time* with a period
(c)   replace *through* with *threw*
(d)   change *missed* to *miss*
(e)   no change is required

9.   Sentence 13: Before you put the article away, write a quick summary, making sure to include the answers to all of your questions.

If you rewrote Sentence 13 beginning with *Making sure to include the answers to all of your questions,* the next words should be

(a)   write a quick
(b)   a quick summary should
(c)   your quick summary
(d)   summarize quick
(e)   one should write

Putting

(1) Even though putting may be the most debated aspect of the game of golf you should follow certain agreed upon procedures. (2) First, stand behind the ball on a line with the cup. (3) From this position, you can estimate the distance of the putt and the slope of the terrain. (4) From there you can also decide how fast the ball should travel. (5) Then walk to different locations on the green to find out if a fresh angle gives you any more information about your putt. (6) Next, assume a comfortible stance over the ball. (7) Grip the club firm, but not tightly, using either a traditional golf grip or a baseball grip. (8) Make sure that the face of the putter is perpendicular to the line that you intend the ball to follow. (9) Before striking the ball, wiggle the club back and forth for relaxation and look up several times at your target. (10) For long putts, who cover most of the green, aim for an area around the hole. (11) For shorter putts, aim for a spot six inches directly behind the hole. (12) As you begin the actual stroke, pull it straight back. (13) With your head down, and your grip tight, strike the ball firmly. (14) Follow through along the line that you hope your ball will follow. (15) Finally, if you miss the putt, make sure that you know why because this information can help you sink future putts.

1. Sentence 1: Even though putting may be the most debated aspect of the game of *golf you* should follow certain agreed upon procedures.

   Which of the following is the best way to write the italicized portion of this sentence? If you think the original is the best way, choose Option (a).

   (a) golf you
   (b) golf. You
   (c) golf You
   (d) golf, you
   (e) golf, You

2. Sentences 3 and 4: From this position, you can estimate the distance of the putt and the slope of the terrain. From there you can also decide how fast the ball should travel.

   The most effective combination of Sentences 3 and 4 would include which of the following groups of words?

(a)   and from there
(b)   but from there
(c)   though from there
(d)   even though from there
(e)   and there

3.   Sentence 5: Then walk to different locations on the green to find out if a fresh angle gives you any more information about your putt.

What correction should be made to this sentence?

(a)   change *Then* to *Than*
(b)   change the spelling of *different* to *differant*
(c)   change the spelling of *angle* to *angel*
(d)   change *gives* to *gave*
(e)   no change is required

4.   Sentence 6: Next, assume a comfortible stance over the ball.

What correction should be made to this sentence?

(a)   remove the comma after *Next*
(b)   change *assume* to *a golfer assumes*
(c)   change the spelling of *comfortible* to *comfortable*
(d)   insert a comma after *stance*
(e)   no change is required

5.   Sentence 7: Grip the club firm, but not tightly, using either a traditional golf grip or a baseball grip.

What correction should be made to this sentence?

(a)   change *firm* to *firmly*
(b)   change *tightly* to *tight*
(c)   change *using* to *use*
(d)   capitalize *baseball*
(e)   no change is required

6.   Sentence 10: For long putts, who cover most of the green, aim for an area around the hole.

What correction should be made to this sentence?

(a) change *who* to *whom*

(b) change *who* to *which*

(c) replace the comma after *green* with a period and capitalize *aim*

(d) change *cover* to *covered*

(e) no change is required

7. Sentence 12: As you begin the actual stroke, pull it straight back.

What correction should be made to this sentence?

(a) change *begin* to *began*

(b) change *it* to *the putter*

(c) replace the comma after *stroke* with a period and capitalize the first letter of *pull*

(d) change the spelling of *straight* to *strait*

(e) no change is required

8. Sentence 13: With your head down, and your grip tight, strike the ball firmly.

What correction should be made to this sentence?

(a) change *your* to *you're*

(b) remove the comma after *tight*

(c) remove the comma after *down*

(d) place a period after *tight* and capitalize the first letter of *strike*

(e) no change is required

9. Sentence 15: Finally, if you miss the putt, make sure that you know why because this information can help you sink future putts.

If you rewrote this as two sentences, the second sentence could begin

(a) This information

(b) The putt

(c) Future putts

(d) Sink

(e) You know

Photography

(1) Taking an engaging picture of an ordinary subject is no easy task, but serious photographers have mastered this skill. (2) Experts realize that because ordinary objects do not attract attention, they have to do something to make these objects seem special. (3) Professionals first considered their choices. (4) They must decide for instance, how far to stand from the subject. (5) They might choose to stand extremely close to something small, even if this short distance require a special lens. (6) Another way photographers make an ordinary subject stand out is to look at it from an unfamiliar angle. (7) They might try snapping the picture from a low vantage point by stooping down. (8) If its possible, they might even shoot from below the object. (9) They could stand on a chair or table to view the object from the top. (10) Yet another way to make an ordinary subject stand out is to photograph only part of it. (11) A typewriter, for example, is not a particularly engaging subject, but the keys alone can be made to look fasinating by a gifted photographer. (12) For a crowd scene, professionals might concentrate on only the feet. (13) The professional is aware of many other choices. (14) These include choices concerning light, how to focus, and type of film. (15) Finally, professionals study their own prints to see what has worked for them in the past.

1. Sentence 1: Taking an engaging picture of an ordinary subject is no easy task, but serious photographers have mastered this skill.

    If you rewrote Sentence 1 beginning with *Although taking an engaging picture of an ordinary subject is no easy task,* the next word(s) should be

    (a)   master
    (b)   serious photographers
    (c)   this skill
    (d)   have mastered
    (e)   but

2. Sentence 3: Professionals first considered their choices.

    What correction should be made to this sentence?

(a) place a comma after *Professionals*
(b) change *considered* to *considering*
(c) change *considered* to *consider*
(d) change *their* to *his*
(e) no change is required

3. Sentence 4: They must *decide for instance, how* far to stand from the subject.

Which of the following is the best way to write the italicized portion of this sentence? If you think the original is the best way, choose Option (a).

(a) decide for instance, how
(b) decide for instance how
(c) decide, for instance how
(d) decide for instance, that
(e) decide, for instance, how

4. Sentence 5: They might choose to stand extremely close to something small, even if *this short distance require* a special lens.

Which of the following is the best way to write the italicized portion of the sentence? If you think the original is the best way, choose Option (a).

(a) this short distance require
(b) this short distance requires
(c) these shorts distances requires
(d) these short distance require
(e) this short distances require

5. Sentence 8: If its possible, they might even shoot from below the object.

What correction should be made to this sentence?

(a) remove the comma after *possible*
(b) replace the final period with a question mark
(c) change *its* to *it's*
(d) change *shoot* to *shot*
(e) no change is required

6. Sentence 10: Yet another way to make an ordinary subject stand out is to photograph only part of it.

What correction should be made to this sentence?

(a)   change the spelling of *ordinary* to *ordinnary*
(b)   change *stand* to *stands*
(c)   change *to make* to *making*
(d)   place *only* before *photograph*
(e)   no change is required

7.   Sentence 11: A typewriter, for example, is not a particularly engaging subject, but the keys alone can be made to look fasinating by a gifted photographer.

What correction should be made to this sentence?

(a)   remove the comma before *for*
(b)   change *keys* to *key's*
(c)   change *made* to *making*
(d)   change the spelling of *fasinating* to *fascinating*
(e)   no change is required

8.   Sentence 14: These include choices concerning light, how to focus, and type of film.

What correction should be made to this sentence?

(a)   change *these* to *this*
(b)   change *how to focus* to *focus*
(c)   place a comma after *type*
(d)   replace the final period with a question mark
(e)   no change is required

9.   Sentence 15: Finally, professionals study their own prints to see what has worked for them in the past.

If you rewrote Sentence 15 beginning with *Finally, to see what has worked for them before*, the next words should be

(a)   prints
(b)   professionals
(c)   the past
(d)   has worked
(e)   they

T.V. News

(1) Television newscasters share many common qualities. (2) Even before viewers turn on the news in New York City or Los Angeles, they can guess whats waiting for them. (3) Instead of a single announcer, they will discover a team of people. (4) This team will consist of an anchorperson, a sportscaster, a weatherperson, and one or two reporters from the field. (5) The anchorperson—whether male or female—will meet the standards of youthful attractiveness set by contemporary advertising. (6) Wouldn't viewers be shocked to see Al Bundy delivering the news. (7) Viewers can feel certain that the anchorperson will report international national and local news in a serious, yet friendly manner. (8) Even friendlier will be the sportscaster, often a former athlete, who will race through the scores of games of national and local significance. (9) Frequent, the sportscaster will conclude by sharing a few predictions concerning upcoming games. (10) Next on the scene will be an equally cheerful meteorologist. (11) This person will joke about storms while pointing at important-looking graphs and charts. (12) Some meteorologist have even come up with their own vocabulary to describe various climatic conditions. (13) Frequently, the news team will bring out a commentator to read an editorial. (14) While starring straight at the camera, this figure will express an opinion about a controversial issue. (15) While this issue could be of national or even international significance, they probably will be a matter that affects local citizens.

1. Sentence 2: Even before viewers turn on the news in New York City or *Los Angeles, they can guess whats* waiting for them.

   Which of the following is the best way to write the italicized portion of the sentence? If you think the original is the best way, choose Option (a).

   (a) Los Angeles, they can guess whats
   (b) Los Angeles they can guess whats
   (c) Los Angeles, they can guess what's
   (d) Los Angeles, you can guess whats
   (e) Los Angeles, they can guess whats'

2. Sentence 3: Instead of a single announcer, they will discover a team of people.

   If you rewrote Sentence 3 beginning with *They will discover,* the sentence should include

   (a) not a single announcer
   (b) not a team of people
   (c) a team and a single announcer
   (d) a team of single announcers
   (e) not people on a team

3. Sentence 6: Wouldn't viewers be shocked to see Al Bundy delivering the news.

   What correction should be made to this sentence?

   (a) change *Wouldn't* to *Would'nt*
   (b) change *Wouldn't* to *Would not*
   (c) change spelling of *shocked* to *schocked*
   (d) replace the period with a question mark
   (e) no change is required

4. Sentence 7: Viewers can feel certain that the anchorperson will report *international national and local news* in a serious, yet friendly manner.

   Which of the following is the best way to write the italicized portion of this sentence? If you think the original is the best way, choose Option (a).

   (a) international national and local news
   (b) international and national and local
   (c) International National and local news
   (d) international, national, and local news
   (e) internationally national and local news

5. Sentence 9: Frequent, the sportscaster will conclude by sharing a few predictions concerning upcoming games.

   What correction should be made to this sentence?

   (a) change *Frequent* to *Frequently*
   (b) remove the comma after *Frequent*
   (c) capitalize the first letter of *sportscaster*
   (d) change *will conclude* to *concluded*
   (e) no change is required

6. Sentence 12: Some meteorologist have even come up with their own vocabulary to describe various climatic conditions.

What correction should be made to this sentence?

(a) change *meteorologist* to *meteorologists*
(b) replace *Some* with *A*
(c) change *their* to *there*
(d) change the spelling of *various* to *varius*
(e) no change is required

7. Sentence 13: Frequently, the news team will bring out a commentator to read an editorial.

What correction should be made to this sentence?

(a) remove the comma after *Frequently*
(b) remove *will*
(c) replace *editorial* with *editorials*
(d) change the spelling of *commentator* to *comentator*
(e) no change is required

8. Sentence 14: While starring straight at the camera, this figure will express an opinion about a controversial issue.

What correction should be made to this sentence?

(a) remove the comma after *camera*
(b) change the spelling of *starring* to *staring*
(c) change *at* to *with*
(d) replace *this* with *these*
(e) no change is required

9. Sentence 15: While this issue could be of national or even international significance, they probably will be a matter that affects local citizens.

What correction should be made to this sentence?

(a) capitalize the first letter of *national* and *international*
(b) remove the comma after *significance*
(c) replace *they* with *it*
(d) change *affects* to *effects*
(e) no change is required

Neckties

(1) Teachers have many more instructional choices than their student realize. (2) This is as true for elementary school teachers as it is for university professors. (3) Even if you are a father teaching your son to tie a necktie, you have a considerable number of teaching strategies to choose from. (4) For example, you could teach by carful modeling. (5) Hear, the two of you should stand side-by-side, each with a tie around his neck. (6) As you tie your tie, your son should follow along, carefully listening to your words and watching your actions. (7) If you preferred, stand behind him and tie the knot for him. (8) Once again, Describe the action of your hands. (9) Because both of these techniques can fail, some fathers have actually resorted to buying their sons instruction books small pamphlets available at clothing stores. (10) If all else fails, you can enlist the help of a patient, neighbor, or friend. (11) Or, you can purchase a clip-on tie and delay the lesson until next year.

1. Sentence 1: Teachers have many more instructional choices *than their student realize.*

   Which of the following is the best way to write the italicized portion of this sentence? If you think the original is the best way, choose Option (a).

   (a) than their student realize.
   (b) then their students realize.
   (c) than her students realize.
   (d) than their student realized.
   (e) than their students realize.

2. Sentence 2: This is as true for elementary school teachers as it is for university professors.

   If you were to rewrite Sentence 2 as two sentences, the second sentence should begin

   (a) This is also true
   (b) This is not as true
   (c) This used to be true
   (d) It can be the case sometimes
   (e) Then it must not be true

3. Sentence 4: For example, you could teach by carful modeling.

   What correction should be made to this sentence?

   (a) remove the comma after *example*
   (b) replace the comma after *example* with a semicolon
   (c) change *you* to *yours*
   (d) change the spelling of *carful* to *careful*
   (e) no change is required

4. Sentence 5: *Hear, the two of you should stand* side-by-side, each with a tie around his neck.

   Which of the following is the best way to write the italicized portion of this sentence? If you think the original is the best way, choose Option (a).

   (a) Hear, the two of you should stand
   (b) Here, the two of you should stand
   (c) Hear the two of you should stand
   (d) Here, the to of you should stand
   (e) Here the two of you standing

5. Sentence 7: If you preferred, stand behind him and tie the knot for him.

   What correction should be made to this sentence?

   (a) remove the comma after *preferred*
   (b) change *preferred* to *prefer*
   (c) change *him* to *he*
   (d) change *knot* to *not*
   (e) no change is required

6. Sentence 8: Once again, Describe the action of your hands.

   What correction should be made to this sentence?

   (a) remove the comma after *again*
   (b) change *Describe* to *describe*
   (c) change *your* to *you*
   (d) change *hands* to *hand's*
   (e) no change is required

7. Sentence 9: Because both of these techniques can fail, some fathers have actually resorted to giving their sons instruction books small pamphlets available at clothing stores.

    What correction should be made to this sentence?

    (a) change the spelling of *techniques* to *techneeks*
    (b) replace the comma after *fail* with a period and capitalize the first letter of *some*
    (c) change *sons* to *sons'*
    (d) insert a comma after *books*
    (e) no change is required

8. Sentence 10: If all else fails, you can enlist the help *of a patient, neighbor, or friend.*

    Which of the following is the best way to write the italicized portion of this sentence? If you think the original is the best way, choose Option (a).

    (a) of a patient, neighbor, or friend
    (b) of a patient neighbor, and friend
    (c) of a patient neighbor or friend
    (d) from a patient, neighbor, or friend
    (e) from a patient neighbor, or friend

9. Sentence 11: Or, you can purchase a clip-on tie and delay the lesson until next year.

    If you rewrote Sentence 11 beginning with *If you want to delay,* the next words should be

    (a) the purchase
    (b) next year
    (c) the lesson
    (d) your purchasing
    (e) a clip-on tie

Health Craze

(1) The new health craze has taken many forms. (2) From dawn until dusk, streets and parks are filled with joggers, one also sees cyclists, roller skaters, walkers, and even people on skis with wheels. (3) Specialized health food stores are common everywhere. (4) And most supermarkets now include entire health food sections. (5) These same stores also sell health lines of soup tea and cereal. (6) In addition to stores that sell health food an increasing number of establishments, especially exercise facilities, sell other health services. (7) On one hand, the traditional gymnasium is more popular than ever as a place to do traditional exercises. (8) On the other, full-service exercise club's feature ultramodern exercise equipment. (9) Along with exercise equipment, these places offer saunas, exercise classes, and even restaurants. (10) Some health clubs even featured full medical counseling programs. (11) For those who want to stay at home to exercise, the oportunities have never been more plentiful. (12) You can buy or rent exercise bicycles, weights, rowing machines, and dozens of other pieces of exercise equipment. (13) You can even buy exercise tapes to play on your video recorder.

1. Sentence 2: From dawn until dusk, streets and parks are filled with *joggers, one* also sees cyclists, roller skaters, walkers, and even people on skis with wheels.

   Which of the following is the best way to write the italicized portion of this sentence? If you think the original is the best way, choose Option (a).

   (a) joggers, one
   (b) joggers one
   (c) joggers. One
   (d) joggers but one
   (e) joggers and one

2. Sentences 3 and 4: Specialized health food stores are common everywhere. And most supermarkets now include entire health food sections.

   The most effective combination of Sentences 3 and 4 would include which of the following groups of words?

(a)   In addition to specialized health food stores, we
(b)   Even though there are specialized
(c)   everywhere, but
(d)   everywhere, even though
(e)   Although specialized food stores

3.   Sentence 5: These same stores also sell health lines of *soup tea and cereal.*

Which of the following is the best way to write the italicized portion of this sentence? If you think the original is the best way, choose Option (a).

(a)   soup tea and cereal.
(b)   soup tea and, cereal.
(c)   soup, tea and, cereal.
(d)   soup, and tea, and cereal.
(e)   soup, tea, and cereal.

4.   Sentence 6: In addition to stores that sell health food an increasing number of establishments, especially exercise facilities, sell other health services.

What correction should be made to this sentence?

(a)   insert a comma after *addition*
(b)   insert a comma after *food*
(c)   remove the comma after *establishments*
(d)   change *sell* to *selling*
(e)   no change is required

5.   Sentence 8: On the other, full-service exercise club's feature ultra-modern exercise equipment.

What correction should be made to this sentence?

(a)   capitalize the first letter of *exercise*
(b)   change *feature* to *featured*
(c)   change *club's* to *clubs'*
(d)   change *club's* to *clubs*
(e)   no change is required

6.   Sentence 10: Some health clubs even featured full medical counseling programs.

What correction should be made to this sentence?

(a)   replace *Some* with *A few*
(b)   place a comma after *clubs*
(c)   change *health clubs* to *Health Clubs*
(d)   change *featured* to *feature*
(e)   no change is required

7.   Sentence 11: For those who want to stay at home to exercise, the oportunities have never been more plentiful.

What correction should be made to this sentence?

(a)   remove the comma after *exercise*
(b)   change the spelling of *oportunities* to *opportunities*
(c)   change *stay* to *remain*
(d)   insert a comma after *more*
(e)   change the spelling of *plentiful* to *plentyfull*

8.   Sentence 12: You can buy or rent exercise bicycles, weights, rowing machines, and dozens of other pieces of exercise equipment.

What correction should be made to this sentence?

(a)   change *You* to *We*
(b)   place a comma after *buy*
(c)   remove comma after *weights*
(d)   change *buy* to *by*
(e)   no change is required

9.   Sentence 13: You can even buy exercise tapes to play on your video recorder.

If you rewrote Sentence 13 beginning with *For your video recorder,* the next word should be

(a)   you
(b)   your
(c)   tapes
(d)   buy
(e)   video

Football

(1) Professional football on television reflects many American values. (2) Our competitive spirit is seen in the intensity of the players, the coaches, and the fans. (3) Clearly, winning is the goal, not competition for it's own sake. (4) Why else would fights occur? (5) At the same time, pro football reflects our respect for law because the referee's word is final, even if his decisions are disputed. (6) To make sure that the right decisions are made, league officials have even allowed officials to rely on filmed replays. (7) Old-fashioned American ingenuity play a big part in professional football just as it does in America's business life. (8) While it's important to have great athletes, it is equally important to have a plan that the opponent has not anticipated. (9) The head Coach, in the great tradition of an American general, deploys his troops in an effort to outflank the enemy. (10) American fans love nothing more then to see this American cleverness win out over apparently invincible odds. (11) Even the commercials reflect our principles by relying so heavy upon the association of American heroes. (12) And lets not forget that professional football is a game. (13) And who loves games more than Americans?

1. Sentence 2: Our competitive spirit is seen in the intensity of the players, the coaches, and the fans.

    If we begin this sentence with *We,* what form of the verb should we use?

    (a) be seen
    (b) is seen
    (c) seeing
    (d) saw that
    (e) can see

2. Sentence 3: Clearly, winning is the *goal, not competition for it's* own sake.

    Which of the following is the best way to write the italicized portion? If you think the original is the best way, choose Option (a).

      (a)   goal, not competition for it's

      (b)   goal, not competition for its

      (c)   goal, not commpetition for it's

      (d)   goal, not competition for its'

      (e)   goal, not commpetition, for its

3. Sentence 7: Old-fashioned American ingenuity play a big part in professional football just as it does in America's business life.

What correction should be made to this sentence?

      (a)   change the spelling of *business* to *bussiness*

      (b)   remove the hyphen from *old-fashioned*

      (c)   replace *play* with *plays*

      (d)   change *it* to *they*

      (e)   no change is required

4. Sentence 8: While it's important to have great athletes, it is equally important to have a plan that the opponent has not anticipated.

What correction should be made to this sentence?

      (a)   change *it's* to *its*

      (b)   change the spelling of *athletes* to *atheletes*

      (c)   remove the comma after *athletes*

      (d)   change the spelling of *equally* to *equaly*

      (e)   no change is required

5. Sentence 9: The head Coach, in the great tradition of an American general, deploys his troops in an effort to out-flank the enemy.

What correction should be made to this sentence?

      (a)   change the spelling of *tradition* to *traddition*

      (b)   do not capitalize *coach*

      (c)   remove the comma after *Coach*

      (d)   replace *deploys* with *deploy*

      (e)   no change is required

6. Sentence 10: American fans love nothing more *then to see this American* cleverness win out over apparently invincible odds.

Which of the following is the best way to write the italicized part of this sentence? If you think the original is the best way, choose Option (a).

(a) then to see this American
(b) then, to see this American
(c) than, to see this American
(d) than to see this American
(e) than to see this american

7. Sentence 11: Even the commericals reflect our principles by relying so heavy upon the association of American heroes.

What correction should be made to this sentence?

(a) change *principles* to *principals*
(b) change *reflect* to *reflects*
(c) change the spelling of *heroes* to *heros*
(d) change *heavy* to *heavily*
(e) no change is required

8. Sentence 12: And lets not forget that professional football is a game.

What correction should be made to this sentence?

(a) change *And* to *But*
(b) change *lets* to *let's*
(c) change *lets* to *lets'*
(d) insert a comma after *football*
(e) no change is required

9. Sentence 13: And who loves games more than Americans?

What correction should be made to this sentence?

(a) change *who* to *whom*
(b) change *who* to *whose*
(c) change *loves* to *love*
(d) replace the question mark with a period
(e) no change is required

Long Trips

(1) While driving along distance alone is never easy, you will enjoy the trip more if you follow a few well-tested tips. (2) Obviously, before you leave, make sure that your car is in good running order by checking the brakes, examining the wiring, and to look at the hoses and anything else that could malfunction. (3) Also, before you start the trip, locate alternate routes on the map. (4) You will then be able to switch to a better road if you encounter a traffic jam. (5) Before you leave, make sure to stock you're car with a variety of audiotapes. (6) Nothing is more irritating than to find yourself driving through the night with only static comming from the radio. (7) And don't forget that you can now purchase or rent tapes of stories. (8) Instede of listening only to music, you can now enjoy the stories of Arthur Conan Doyle or the novels of Stephen King. (9) If you are not in a hurry, add variety to your trip by leaving the main highway from time to time to drive along a less-traveled road. (10) What better way is there to learn local history and customs. (11) Finally, make sure that you drove carefully. (12) Nothing are more exhausting or more dangerous than to drive in a fatigued state of mind. (13) No trip is important enough to risk your life.

1. Sentence 1: While driving *along distance alone is never easy,* you will enjoy the trip more if you follow a few well-tested tips.

    Which of the following is the best way to write the italicized portion of this sentence? If you think the original is the best way, choose Option (a).

    (a)   along distance alone is never easy,
    (b)   a long distance alone is never easy
    (c)   a long distance alone is never easy;
    (d)   along distance alone is never easy;
    (e)   a long distance alone is never easy,

2. Sentence 2: Obviously, before you leave, make sure that your car is in good running order by checking the brakes, examining the wiring, *and to look at the hoses and* anything else that could malfunction.

    Which of the following is the best way to write the italicized portion of the sentence? If you think the original is the best way, choose Option (a).

(a)   and to look at the hoses and
(b)   and to look to the hoses or
(c)   and looking at the hoses and
(d)   or looking at the hoses or
(e)   or look at the hoses and

3.   Sentences 3 and 4: Also, before you start the trip, locate alternate routes on the map. You will then be able to switch to a better road if you encounter a traffic jam.

    The most effective combination of Sentences 3 and 4 would include which of the following groups of words?

    (a)   because you will then
    (b)   even though with a traffic jam
    (c)   despite a better route
    (d)   because of a traffic jam
    (e)   since traffic encounters

4.   Sentence 5: Before you *leave, make sure to stock you're car* with a variety of audiotapes.

    Which of the following is the best way to write the italicized portion of this sentence? If you think the original is the best way, choose Option (a).

    (a)   leave, make sure to stock you're car
    (b)   leave, make sure to stock your car
    (c)   leave make sure to stock your car
    (d)   leave, make sure also to stock you're car,
    (e)   leave make sure to stock your car,

5.   Sentence 6: Nothing is more irritating than to find yourself driving through the night with only static comming from the radio.

    What correction should be made to this sentence?

    (a)   insert a comma after *irritating*
    (b)   change the spelling of *irritating* to *iritating*
    (c)   change *than* to *then*
    (d)   change spelling of *comming* to *coming*
    (e)   no change is required

6.   Sentence 8: Instede of listening only to music, you can now enjoy the stories of Arthur Conan Doyle or the novels of Stephen King.

What correction should be made to this sentence?

(a)   change the spelling of *Instede* to *Instead*
(b)   remove the comma after *music*
(c)   replace *can now enjoy* with *enjoyed*
(d)   capitalize the first letter of *novels*
(e)   no change is required

7.   Sentence 10: What better way is there to learn local history and customs.

What correction should be made to this sentence?

(a)   change *there* to *their*
(b)   place a comma after *history*
(c)   capitalize the first letter in the word *history*
(d)   replace the period after *customs* with a question mark
(e)   no change is required

8.   Sentence 11: Finally, make sure that you drove carefully.

What correction should be made to this sentence?

(a)   remove the comma after *Finally*
(b)   change *drove* to *driving*
(c)   change *drove* to *drive*
(d)   change *carefully* to *careful*
(e)   no change is required

9.   Sentence 12: Nothing are more exhausting or more danger-ous than to drive in a fatigued state of mind.

What correction should be made to this sentence?

(a)   change *exhausting* to *exausting*
(b)   replace *are* with *is*
(c)   change *than* to *then*
(d)   replace *to* with *too*
(e)   place a question mark after *mind*

Computers

(1) How can computers help us? (2) According to the advertisements, they can helping us throughout the day. (3) Some of these commercials even suggest that students without computers will fail in school and that families without computers will end up impoverished. (4) While computers are not the miracle machines the companies sometimes claim, computers do, in fact, help people in several important ways. (5) If writing is part of your job, for example, you will probably write better with a word processor. (6) This machine will allow you to correct misteaks during the writing process. (7) Having this capablility means that you can continue to improve your essay without having to spend additional time recopying what you have already completed. (8) A word processor is also a valuable tool because it gives you the power to move words, sentences, and even entire paragraphs to different locations in your composition. (9) With this capacity, you can experiment with new designs without sacrificing much time. (10) In addition to helping you write a computer can offer recreation. (11) For the young, there is diverting video games and ingenious search challenges. (12) For the slightly older, computer baseball and computer chess offer hours of enjoyment. (13) Any age group used the computer to learn a new skill. (14) From a computer, you can learn how to type, how to balance a checking account, and even how to use a computer.

1. Sentence 2: According to the *advertisements, they can helping* us throughout the day.

   Which of the following is the best way to write the italicized portion of this sentence? If you think the original is the best way, choose Option (a).

   (a)   advertisements, they can helping
   (b)   advertisements, they have help
   (c)   advertisements. They helped
   (d)   advertisements, they can help
   (e)   advertisements. They help

2. Sentence 3: Some of these commercials even suggest that students without computers will fail in school and that families without computers will end up impoverished.

   An effective way to make Sentence 3 into two sentences would include which combination of words?

       (a)   Other commercials suggest
       (b)   Other commercials deny
       (c)   Other colleges tell us
       (d)   Families on welfare claim
       (e)   Computers fail

3. Sentence 5: If writing is part of your *job, for example, you* will probably write better with a word processor.

Which of the following is the best way to write the italicized portion of this sentence? If you think the original is the best way, choose Option (a).

    (a)   job, for example, you
    (b)   job for example you
    (c)   job for example, you
    (d)   job, for example, one
    (e)   job. For example, you

4. Sentence 6: This machine will allow you to correct misteaks during the writing process.

What correction should be made to this sentence?

    (a)   change *allow* to *allowing*
    (b)   insert a comma after *misteaks*
    (c)   change the spelling of *misteaks* to *mistakes*
    (d)   change the period after *process* to a comma
    (e)   no change is required

5. Sentence 9: With this capacity, you can experiment with new designs without sacrificing much time.

What correction should be made to this sentence?

    (a)   remove the comma after *capacity*
    (b)   remove *can*
    (c)   change the spelling of *experiment* to *expariment*
    (d)   change *you can experiment* to *one can experiment*
    (e)   no change is required

6. Sentence 10: In addition to helping you write a computer can offer recreation.

What correction should be made to this sentence?

(a)   change *In addition* to *Inaddition*
(b)   insert a comma after *write*
(c)   insert a comma after *computer*
(d)   change the spelling of *offer* to *ofer*
(e)   no change is required

7.   Sentence 11: For the young, there is diverting video games and ingenious search challenges.

What correction should be made to this sentence?

(a)   change *for* to *four*
(b)   change *there* to *their*
(c)   replace *is* with *are*
(d)   insert a comma after *games*
(e)   no change is required

8.   Sentence 13: Any age group used the computer to learn a new skill.

What correction should be made to this sentence?

(a)   Change *Any* to *Few*
(b)   change *used* to *can use*
(c)   change the spelling of *group* to *groop*
(d)   insert a comma after *learn*
(e)   no change is required

9.   Sentence 14: From a computer, you can learn how to type, how to balance a checking account, and even how to use a computer.

If you rewrote Sentence 14 beginning with *A computer can teach you,* the next word should be

(a)   that
(b)   when
(c)   how
(d)   since
(e)   if

Answer Key

page 42	page 43	page 44	page 45
Part One	**Part Two**	**Part Three**	**Part Four**
1. e	1. b	1. b	1. e
2. a	2. d	2. a	2. b
3. c	3. c	3. c	3. a
4. b	4. a	4. a	4. c
5. d	5. e	5. b	5. b
6. c	6. b	6. c	6. a

page 46	page 47	page 48
Part Five	**Part Six**	**Part Seven**
1. s	1. c	1. b
2. a	2. d	2. f
3. s	3. b	3. d
4. a	4. e	4. e
5. a	5. b	5. a
6. s	6. a	6. c

page 68
Exercise 1

1. Rewrite: Before examinations, George does not eat well.
   Rule No. 6: Use adjectives and adverbs correctly.
2. Rewrite: Bill's brother, a huge man, used to play professional football.
   Rule No. 10: Punctuate correctly.
3. Rewrite: Lie down on the ground, Bowser, so that I can clean your paws.
   Rule No. 5: Use the correct form of verbs.
4. Rewrite: Neither of the girls is fond of pizza.
   Rule No. 2: Make subjects and verbs agree in number.
5. Rewrite: Are the ladies and gentlemen at that table all ready to order?
   Rule No. 8: Do not confuse words that are similar in spelling or pronunciation.
6. Rewrite: Every one of the men spent several hours working in his own garden.
   Rule No. 3: Make pronouns agree with their antecedents.
7. Rewrite: Mr. Bolivar prefers to read, to exercise, and to play piano.
   Rule No. 7: Construct equal elements of a sentence in parallel form.

8. Rewrite: Many people living in the South like to eat grits.
   Rule No. 9: Capitalize correctly.
9. Rewrite: The elderly woman gave the ice cream to Dorothy and me.
   Rule No. 4: Use the correct case of personal pronouns.
10. Rewrite: While Bob was away, the cat ran off with his slippers.
   Rule No. 1: Use complete sentences; avoid fragments and run-ons.

page 69
Exercise 2

1. Rewrite: Meagan plays regularly with the Baldino children.
   Rule No. 6: Use adjectives and adverbs correctly.
2. Rewrite: Letitia's favorite season of the year is spring.
   Rule No. 9: Capitalize correctly.
3. Rewrite: The booster club held an election to select its officers.
   Rule No. 3: Make pronouns agree with their antecedents.
4. Rewrite: Both of the golfers have had a low score.
   Rule No. 2: Make subjects and verbs agree in number.
5. Rewrite: According to many campers, rafting is better than canoeing.
   Rule No. 7: Construct equal elements of a sentence in parallel form.
6. Rewrite: Vijay enjoys the great outdoors. Helen prefers libraries and bookstores.
   Rule No. 1: Use complete sentences; avoid fragments and run-ons.
7. Rewrite: It was I whose poor play cost us the game.
   Rule No. 4: Use the correct case of personal pronouns.
8. Rewrite: Shouting and stamping his feet, the toddler refused to get ready for bed.
   Rule No. 10: Punctuate correctly.
9. Rewrite: After high school, Derek led a solitary life.
   Rule No. 5: Use the correct form of verbs.
10. Rewrite: Rowena has trouble accepting compliments.
   Rule No. 8: Do not confuse words that are similar in spelling or pronunciation.

page 72 Pressure	page 75 Reading	page 78 Putting	page 81 Photography
1. b	1. b	1. d	1. b
2. a	2. a	2. a	2. c
3. e	3. c	3. e	3. e
4. c	4. a	4. c	4. b
5. c	5. e	5. a	5. c
6. e	6. a	6. b	6. e
7. a	7. c	7. b	7. d
8. b	8. e	8. c	8. b
9. c	9. a	9. a	9. b

page 84
TV News
1. c
2. a
3. d
4. d
5. a
6. a
7. e
8. b
9. c

page 87
Neckties
1. e
2. a
3. d
4. b
5. b
6. b
7. d
8. c
9. c

page 90
Health Craze
1. c
2. e
3. e
4. b
5. d
6. d
7. b
8. e
9. a

page 93
Football
1. c
2. b
3. c
4. e
5. b
6. d
7. d
8. b
9. e

page 96
Long Trips
1. e
2. c
3. a
4. b
5. d
6. a
7. d
8. c
9. b

page 99
Computers
1. d
2. a
3. a
4. c
5. e
6. b
7. c
8. b
9. c